THE
FRANKIES SPUNTINO

Kitchen Companion
& Cooking Manual

An Illustrated Guide to "*Simply the Finest*"

FRANK FALCINELLI, FRANK CASTRONOVO,
AND PETER MEEHAN

DESIGN BY TRAVIS LEE KAUFFMAN
ILLUSTRATIONS BY SARAH RUTHERFORD

ARTISAN
New York

Published by Artisan
A Division of Workman Publishing Company, Inc.
225 Varick Street
New York, NY 10014-4381
www.artisanbooks.com

Published simultaneously in Canada by Thomas Allan & Son, Limited.

Library of Congress Cataloging-in-Publication Data

Falcinelli, Frank.
The Frankies Spuntino kitchen companion & cooking manual / by Frank Falcinelli,
Frank Castronovo, and Peter Meehan.
p. cm.
Includes index.
ISBN 978-1-57965-415-3
1. Cookery, Italian. 2. Cookery, American.
3. Frankies Spuntino (Restaurants)
I. Castronovo, Frank. II. Meehan, Peter, 1977– III. Title.
TX723.F33143 2010
641.5945—dc22   2009048964

Design by Travis Lee Kauffman
Illustrations by Sarah Rutherford

Printed in China

3 5 7 9 10 8 6 4 2

Merlin

To our grandmothers

FRANK FALCINELLI

FRANK CASTRONOVO

CONTENTS

Preface x

Introduction xiv

About These Recipes & This Cooking...........................xix

1. Equipment & Pantry....................................... 1

2. Antipasto...25

3. Sandwiches & Soups....................................55

4. Salads 65

5. Pasta..89

6. Meats & Other Main Courses 123

7. Sunday Sauce 151

8. Desserts...165

Appendices 179

Acknowledgments 213

Index...219

The Frankies Crest...234

PREFACE

I didn't immediately recognize the number but I picked up anyway.
It was a voice out of my past: Frank Falcinelli.

We'd met during my brief, unsatisfying, and unsuccessful turn in the public relations business. (I was twenty-two and didn't really understand what
"public relations" was.) He was the chef at a place called Moomba, which
scored two stars from Ruth Reichl in *The New York Times*. But by the time the
PR firm I was working for got hired by the restaurant, the food had become
an afterthought to the lounge upstairs, a fiercely guarded den of sin for models and celebrities.

We hung out a couple of times, had a couple of good nights. Frank eventually moved out west to open a Moomba in Los Angeles, and I thought
that was the end of it. Then, boom, five or six years later a vaguely familiar
917 number pops up on my cell phone. Frank Falcinelli. He tells me he has
opened a new place in Brooklyn.

I knew all that: my colleague, Dana Bowen, with whom I shared stew-
ardship of *The New York Times* "$25 & Under" restaurant column for a spell,
had written a glowing review of the restaurant Frankies Spuntino, which
Falcinelli had opened with another guy named Frank, his partner and co-chef
Frank Castronovo.

For me, it was halfway curious to see Falcinelli's name, which I had vaguely
associated with Asian–New American food, attached to a homey Italian-
American spot in Brooklyn (though with a name like Falcinelli, it shouldn't

have been a surprise). Come check it out, he said, and he added some bait: there was going to be a party, with a bonfire in the back garden and Chris Robinson from the Black Crowes spinning records. I hadn't been listening to a ton of Black Crowes at that point, but "Sometimes Salvation" was the first song I ever played onstage, back at a guitar showcase when I was fifteen, so that sounded like a good time. And who doesn't like a bonfire? Why not go see what Frank was up to?

It was a great night. Frank had mellowed in the intervening years and ditched the whole Moomba scene. He and Castronovo were trying to create a restaurant that was welcoming, unpretentious, and warm. And it was, genuinely so.

Soon after, I went back to the Spuntino for dinner. Falcinelli describes the food that he and Castronovo serve as the "lighter side of Italian cooking," in the sardonically cornball way he likes to brand everything (like calling this book "An Illustrated Guide to 'Simply the Finest'"; or proclaiming that "Every day is Sunday" at the Spuntino).

I was skeptical of the conceit—maybe of Italian-American restaurants in general, after too many lackluster meals. But there was a curious ingenuity to the Franks' take on Italian-American cooking—a lot of subtraction where other chefs would add, restraint where others would let loose.

Their avoidance of fried food seemed like a bad idea to me at first, but I realized that the more healthful approach made even the most indulgent classics that much more gentle. The Franks larded their menu with many of the nostalgic dishes that they had grown up with, including braciola, the cheese-stuffed braised pork shoulder that's a hallmark of every red-sauce joint in Brooklyn. But their versions were lighter, easier to eat, and impossible not to crave. They were not so much reimagined as reconsidered.

In the years since I first trekked out to Brooklyn to visit the Spuntino, I've eaten an acre's worth of the Franks' Eggplant Marinara and probably made enough of their Caesar salad dressing to fill a claw-foot tub. I initially thought the white pepper they use, almost exclusively, was a strange affectation (a relic of their professional training in France), but now that I've tested their recipes over and over again in my own kitchen, I find that it's the pepper grinder I reach for most often no matter what I'm making.

This cookbook was a slow and natural outgrowth of our developing friendship.

Over the years, I got to know both Franks better and their families, too: some of my favorite afternoons of the past few years were spent out at the beer garden with the gun range on Long Island with Falcinelli's now 100-year-old grandfather, who's sharper than either his grandson or me, and with Castronovo and his wife, Heike, who's from the Black Forest of Germany, and their two kids, who are eternally tolerant and beatifically patient compared to what I was like at their ages.

Through the Spuntino, I also got to know Tony Durazzo, who's an architectural engineer by trade, and helped the guys design and build their restaurants, but who is more importantly a talismanic presence, a connection to the Italian-Americanness of Carroll Gardens (where Tony grew up and where the Spuntino is located), to all kinds of aspects of hippie life in the 1960s and 1970s (which Tony lived), and, most importantly, to some really good food (like Tony's recipe for Spuntino Meatballs, which is from his mom, on page 127). I also bonded with Travis Kauffman, the soft-spoken son of Michigan Mennonites, who designed books before getting mixed up (and eventually becoming a partner in) the restaurants.

It was Travis's idea to create an embossed, gilded, faux-leather cover for this cookbook, with hand-drawn illustrations of everything from can openers to ravioli. I was trying to figure out the angle to take on the text when I ran into Michael Klausman, who I met that first night I went out to Frankies, the evening of the bonfire and the hang. Michael was playing records that night, too—he and Chris always did the nights at the Spuntino together—and we got to know each other over the next few months because he worked at Other Music, a record store where I spend a disproportionate amount of my income. I'd routinely go in, and he'd hip me to the latest reissues of folk records and other weird sounds, usually from the quiet, downer fringe.

One Saturday I was there to pick up some music, and he dropped a bomb on me: he and his girlfriend were unexpectedly pregnant. He asked me, as a food guy, about books to buy and what to cook—he and his girl had to start counting their pennies and he had to build up some dad skills. The Franks and I were already sketching out the recipes for this book, and I knew Michael liked their restaurant.

The thing: it would have been the perfect book for him then and there. The more I had learned about the Franks' cooking at the Spuntino, the more truth I discovered in what they had told me was their secret: It's that their cooking is dead simple. No extra steps or flourishes; this is one-pan and one-pot food, and that's for the really complicated stuff. With a grinder full of white pepper and access to a decent Italian grocery, there's nothing between these covers that's beyond the skills of an absolute novice. And there are plenty of dishes—like Meatballs for the meat eaters or the Eggplant Marinara—that work well for a group, but, revisited a couple of times over the course of a couple of days, could sustain a couple that doesn't have time to cook dinner every night. The Caesar Salad should outrage traditionalists in print but please the cook with its ease and make everybody happy on the plate.

It was going to be a great starter cookbook for a guy in Michael's position: somebody who needed a companion to show him and his girlfriend around the kitchen and supply a few well-tested recipes, the kind that everybody likes (because everybody likes tomato sauce).

I didn't have it then—instead I brought him a few huge cans of La Valle tomatoes, like they use at Frankies, and some good dried pasta. But I've got it now. This book is for anyone who needs ideas for some good, easy meals—for eating every day, for raising a family on, for entertaining friends and pleasing everybody. A little late for Michael, perhaps, but maybe not for you.

—pfm, 2010

INTRODUCTION

The cops were searching Frank Castronovo's car. (It's a long story.)

It was the summer of 2003, on one of those blessedly nice days with a good breeze and a clear blue sky. Frank Falcinelli was sitting on the windowsill of his second-floor Greenwich Village apartment spacing out, playing his guitar poorly.

His apartment overlooked the corner where Commerce Street makes an abrupt hairpin turn, creating a quiet nook cradled by handsome low-rise brick buildings. It was quiet, but not at the moment, because there was a guy getting hassled by the cops across the street, who were busting his chops over something and poking around his car.

They searched the car, high and low, back and front, but didn't find anything. Frank Castronovo told them he was on a bread run—heading over to Sullivan Street Bakery to get bread for Parrish & Company, the restaurant where he was the chef. And as they lost interest, he noticed the guy who'd been watching the whole scene unfold, the guy in the window.

Those crazy blue eyes. He'd only known one person in his life with eyes like that. They'd grown up together in Queens Village in New York City. They'd played street hockey. Knew each other from around. As the cops peeled off, Castronovo turned around and gave a shout: "Yo, what's up, Frank?" He got a weird stare back. "Frank," Castronovo pressed, "what's up? It's Frank from Queens Village."

It had been eighteen years since they'd last seen each other, at a cheesy Long Island bar called the Malibu in 1985. They had a lot to catch up on.

In the nearly two decades since they'd last met, the Franks—the plural-but-not-possessive Franks of the Frankies Spuntino restaurants—had both become chefs, building separate but equally ironclad résumés.

As young men, both had trained in France, Falcinelli mastering confit in the Michelin-starred kitchens of Toulouse and Gascony, Castronovo interning at Paul Bocuse's legendary flagship restaurant in Lyon. Back in New York, in the late 1980s and early 1990s, they'd each worked under some of the

biggest chefs of the era—David Bouley and Charlie Palmer among them—
before running their own kitchens at a number of well-regarded downtown
Manhattan spots, including Moomba and Bistro Jean-Claude.

But in 2003, when they reconnected so randomly on Commerce Street,
both men were approaching their forties and feeling the burnout that comes
with a couple of decades spent in restaurant kitchens. The novelty of all those
fancy ingredients, the charm of those heavy French sauces and sparkle of
imported Asian condiments—all staples of their cooking to that point—had
started to wear thin. Oats sowed and stars earned and mountains climbed—
they were spent, shot.

It wasn't long—a few weeks of hanging out and reconnecting and figur-
ing out that they knew a million people in common—before Falcinelli told
Castronovo about a plan he had in the works. After years of toiling in professional kitchens, he wanted to return to his roots—to the roots they shared—
and revisit the Italian-American cuisine they'd grown up on, back when every
Sunday meant a visit to Grandma's house and a huge spread of the Sunday
Sauce.

The Sunday Sauce, for the uninitiated, is a huge pot of tomato sauce that's
been used to turn tough, cheap meat into a tender, delicious dinner and that
has, in the exchange, been made richer and deeper by all the commingled
simmering. But it's also the name for what augments that meat and sauce—
bread and pasta, salads and antipasti, and cannoli from the bakery—and the
name for the whole experience.

Finding the right location was essential. Manhattan was too expensive,
too overblown. It had to be Brooklyn. And in fact, Falcinelli already had a
line on the perfect spot: a tin-ceilinged old tenement building in tree-lined
Carroll Gardens, complete with an old horse stable and a garden with a
view of the elevated F train whizzing past in the distance. The address was
457 Court Street.

Lease in hand, the Franks set out to build a restaurant with a fresher, less
gimmicky approach to Italian-Americanness. No checkered tablecloths, no
pictures of Grandma Brooklyn on the wall, no deep-fried crap that will send
Uncle Everybody scrambling for pink relief in the medicine cabinet in the
hours after dinner. They set out to restore the old space, scraping clean the
paint-riddled pressed-tin ceiling and commissioning an antique-style bar to
be custom-carved out of mahogany. Then they scrapped every dated flourish
from the frozen-in-time school of Italianate restaurant design. On the speak-
ers, Caruso was out, replaced by Neil Young and the Grateful Dead. Red-

and-white tablecloths were vanquished in favor of simple wood tables. The end result was a restaurant that managed to be both friendly and hip, with a backyard that was good for bonfires in winter and long days of drinking pink wine in summer.

Tradition is tradition for a reason, and messing with it isn't always smart. But the Franks took their decades of experience and brought it to bear on the homey cooking of their youth. Step one was to lighten everything up: heartburn is fine for memories but hard when you have to get up the next morning. Their meatballs are baked instead of fried; gentle simmering takes precedence over hard sautéing. They also expanded their repertory beyond red-sauce cuisine to include salads and simply cooked vegetables that were more than just an afterthought aimed at somebody's dieting aunt.

The menu was designed to be simple enough to be mostly assembled in the restaurant's tiny open kitchen located alongside the long and narrow dining room. They decided that there would be no overhead vent sucking up the fumes of what was cooking and filling their dining room with a low, humming din. According to the strictures of New York City's fire code, that meant they couldn't have a gas range in the kitchen. So they invested in induction burners, cooking tools that use magnets instead of flames to heat pans—known to anybody in the high-end catering game: put your hand on one, it's cold; put the right kind of pot on it and water will boil in mere minutes. The original Spuntino had one oven in the basement, a couple of toaster ovens, a few

Induction Burner

induction burners, and that was it. There was going to be no flash or flame to making the food work.

When they had the plan together, it was around Thanksgiving, and Falcinelli was at his grandmother Anne Martucci's house, describing his new—and first Italian-American—venture. It seemed like the most original idea in the world to him: small plates, a menu where a carpenter from the neighborhood could have a sandwich and beer for less than $15, and where you could bring your daughter to get married in the backyard for a day of celebration. His grandmother, who loved the idea, said, "Oh, so what you're doing is opening a spuntino?"

A Spuntino. A snack or a place to eat them. And a new vocabulary word for the Franks. With that last brick in place, they had a name, a mission, an animating breath of life. Frankies 457 Court Street Spuntino was born.

FRANKIES SPUNTINO
457 COURT STREET
BROOKLYN, NY 11231

ABOUT THESE RECIPES
& THIS COOKING

The recipes contained herein are a more-or-less complete core catalog of the dishes that have been served at the Spuntino since it opened in 2004 (and at its Manhattan sibling, which opened in 2006).

It's a short roster of dishes that Frank and Frank like to think of as greatest hits—dishes that everybody likes, unbound by any strictures like whether or not they're particularly Italian American. (Caesar salad and crème brulée aren't, but everybody wants to eat them, so what's there to argue about?)

The recipes in this book are easy. Easy to imagine why you want to eat them. Easy to cook, but more than that, easy to prepare in a low-stress way in any home kitchen. Plus, almost every dish is cheap from a buying-ingredients perspective. The go-to cheese is Pecorino Romano, a third of the cost of Parmesan. Except for one rib-eye recipe, everything is ground meat, shoulders, and other affordable cuts. The core of the Spuntino's cooking is everyday Italian-American cooking, and that style developed during lean times. (And, without attributing too much grace to it, it also helps to keep their restaurant affordable and appealing.)

Most of the work-work in their recipes—the part where you mess up your counters and floor and generally feel like cursing—happens well before you serve the food, so by the time you *are* ready to serve, you can ladle it out and pretend like it was no problem and you could do it any old time. It's a strategy that came about both as a result of the limited space and equipment they had in their own restaurant kitchen, and as a legacy of all those formative Sunday meals they experienced growing up. Grandma never broke a sweat (or you certainly never saw it). Neither should you.

TOMATO SAUCE

Escoffier codified the mother sauces of French cooking. In the Italian-American tradition, there is only one: tomato sauce. Call it marinara (we do), call it gravy (we don't), call it whatever your grandma called it. It's tomato sauce. There's almost nothing we won't cook in it or put it on.

The real deal—what we grew up with and the way we would do it if we had our choice (and didn't have so many vegetarian friends and customers) would be to make that sauce, then simmer up a batch of braciola or meatballs in it, and then use the resulting meat-infused product as our "tomato sauce" in all its myriad applications. And if you're not catering to vegetarians, we advise doing just that: make a triple batch of sauce, use it to simmer up braciola or meatballs (or any of the other dishes suggested on pages 134–39) and then use that tomato sauce, fresh or from the freezer, whenever tomato sauce is called for in these pages.

Use good Italian canned tomatoes and high quality olive oil when making this sauce, and take your time—there's no rushing it. When you're cooking the garlic, you want to very, very slowly convert the starches in it to sugars and then to caramelize those sugars. Slow and steady. (See the picture of perfectly cooked garlic in the photo section for reference.) Then get the tomatoes in and let them simmer. Not a ton happens over the four hours—no epic deepening of color or furious reduction—but it cooks as much water out of the tomatoes as possible without turning them into tomato paste.

1. Combine the olive oil and garlic in a large deep saucepan and cook over medium-low heat for about 10 minutes, stirring or swirling occasionally, until the garlic is deeply colored—striations of deep brown running through golden cloves—and fragrant. If the garlic starts to smell acrid or sharp or is taking on color quickly, pull the pan off the stove and reduce the heat.

2. While the garlic is getting golden, deal with the tomatoes: Pour them into a bowl and crush them with your hands. We like to pull out the firmer stem end from each of the tomatoes as we crush them and discard those along with the basil leaves that are packed into the can.

3. When the garlic is just about done, add the red pepper flakes to the oil and cook them for 30 seconds or a minute, to infuse their flavor and spice into the oil. Dump in the tomatoes, add the salt, and stir well. Turn the heat up to medium, get the sauce simmering at a gentle pace, not aggressively, and simmer for 4 hours. Stir it from time to time. Mother it a little bit.

4. Check the sauce for salt at the end. The sauce can be cooked with meat at this point, or stored, covered, in the fridge for at least 4 days or frozen for up to a few months.

Makes about 3 quarts

1 cup olive oil

13 whole cloves garlic, peeled

One 96-ounce can (or, if you can find it, 1-kg) or four 28-ounce cans Italian tomatoes

Large pinch of red pepper flakes

2 teaspoons fine sea salt, plus more to taste

CHAPTER 1

EQUIPMENT & PANTRY

EQUIPMENT

The type of food we cook at the Spuntino is not complicated. You've probably got enough equipment on hand to make most of it right now. But there are a few tools that make it easier.

The Spuntino Starter Kit would include the knife set we prescribe herein, a gigantic sturdy mixing bowl, two pepper mills, a heavy-bottomed pot for boiling water and another for simmering the sauce.

A colander to drain the pasta is good to have, as is a wooden spoon to stir the sauce. It's nice to keep a vegetable peeler around, but this food is rustic and simple enough so that you'll get by just fine if you don't.

A standing electric mixer that kneads pasta dough, whips egg whites, and creams butter is a serious time saver. KitchenAid mixers are our favorite. When we sneak a peek into friends' kitchens and discover a KitchenAid mixer, we know they must be serious. (Sometimes more serious about having the latest cobalt-blue mixer than actually knowing how to use it, but we're still happy to see them. Over the years we've had countless mixers fry out—like when a prep cook decides to double a pasta recipe and kills the motor—and knowing that you've got a friend with an unused shiny blue mixer that you can borrow is very reassuring.)

Grandma used her hands to make pasta and a whisk to whip cream, though, so I guess if you were going to throw something essential overboard, it would be the mixer—but that makes having a big cutting board or at the very least a very big slab of wood essential. In most Italian family kitchens, this board would double as a cutting station and a place to mix, cut, and shape pasta.

Once you have the basics, it's very nice to embellish the collection with a cavatelli maker and a pasta machine.

In short: It doesn't take much gear to make this sort of food. The equipment list is short, but the more tools you have from this chapter, the easier it will be to prepare the dishes in the book. More ease, less stress.

BLENDER

Vita-Mix is the first and last name in blenders. Every part is heavy-duty: the motor, the bearings, the power transfer station, and even the bushings. The lowest-end model Vita-Mix is the highest-end blender you could ever need at home. It will last forever.

Vita-Mix Blender

We use blenders to emulsify our vinaigrettes until they've got a silky sheen. While you don't need a Vita-Mix to make salad dressing, we don't think you'll ever regret buying one. Make sure to wash it well after each use; you don't want to go on a health kick and start making smoothies that taste like Caesar salad.

BOX GRATER/MICROPLANE

Our grandmas had box graters; our grandfathers had Microplanes, except they were called rasps and weren't used for shredding cheese.

Frankly, if we were to have only one, it would be the box grater: the coarseness that even the fine side lends the cheese creates an appealing, old-world texture perfect for stuffing inside lasagna or a batch of meatballs or scattering over a plate of pasta.

Microplane   *Box Grater*

But Microplanes are way better for grating the zest off citrus for cheesecakes and the like. You get all aromatic skin and no bitter white pith. They're also excellent for when you want really, really finely grated, fluffy light cheese, like when it's going over a salad.

Get one of each. They're not expensive. And pay attention to graters: they get dull, and dull graters are how you end up retexturing your knuckles. Replace any dull tool that's supposed to be sharp.

CAN OPENER

Not a lot to say here, other than that electric ones are for cat ladies. And without one, you're going to have a hell of a time opening all the cans of San Marzano tomatoes you need for our recipes.

Can Opener

CAVATELLI MAKER

You feed a snake of dough in one side, turn the crank, and cavatelli spit out of the other. A brilliant invention. BeeBo cavatelli makers—our brand of choice—were first made by the Berarducci Brothers Manufacturing Company of McKeesport, Pa. The Berarduccis made cavatelli makers

(and ravioli molds and tomato squeezers and all kinds of stuff) through the middle of the last century and then sold the design and name to Ohio-based VillaWare. Unfortunately, VillaWare stopped making the BeeBo in 2008. (We only found out while working on this book.) Fortunately, other cavatelli makers on the market these days are nearly exact copies. Look for models with wooden rollers, which are preferable to plastic ones, or look on eBay for vintage BeeBos—they come up all the time. One thing's for sure: we would never make cavatelli without one. Our cavatelli recipe—which we learned from the pamphlet in the BeeBo box—is on page 100.

Cavatelli Maker

CUTTING BOARD

We like wooden cutting boards for dry stuff: cutting pasta, slicing bread, and any flour-based pastry projects. We like machine-washable boards for everything else. Why? Wood is absorbent. Would you cut raw meat on your telephone book?

Wood Cutting Board

KNIVES

There have been countless times—cooking at friends' apartments or somebody's rented beach house—that we've made do with nothing more than a set of cheap plastic-handled serrated knives purchased as part of an apartment starter set. But if you're serious about cooking, having a few good knives is nice.

The rules for buying knives: avoid buying a department store set. (If you already have one, the rule is to keep them sharp.) Buy your knives one at a time and get to know a little about the knife you bought. Familiarize yourself with its characteristics—the thickness of the blade, the weight, etc.—and then use your impressions of that knife to inform the next purchase. Decide whether you want the next knife that you buy to be shorter, longer, heavier, whatever. Carbon steel blades are great—they take a good edge. But if you're careless (meaning you don't clean and dry your knives conscientiously), they

will rust. Stainless steel won't rust no matter how badly you treat it.

You might stick with one brand, or you may shop around. If there's a cookware store near you that will let you handle the knives, to feel them in your hands before purchasing, shop there and test out a lot of blades. Never just buy a knife because it's expensive. Figure out what you want in a knife and then go shopping for that.

The big three:

An **8-inch** or **10-inch chef's knife** is good for all general chopping, slicing, and any vegetable cuts (medium dice, fine dice, etc.), and the side of the knife is good for crushing cloves of garlic. A chef's knife that's shorter than 8 inches is no good, because you have to rock up high to make your cuts, and anything longer than 10 inches is too long—too hard to sharpen evenly. Excellent, however, as a comedy prop.

A **serrated knife** is necessary for slicing bread and great for slicing tomatoes. No point in living without one. Offset serrated knives (there's a kink where the blade meets the handle, giving you better leverage over the large blade) are a good choice.

A **paring knife** is there for shaping vegetables (trimming off unwanted bits, squaring off vegetables so they will be easier to cut with your chef's

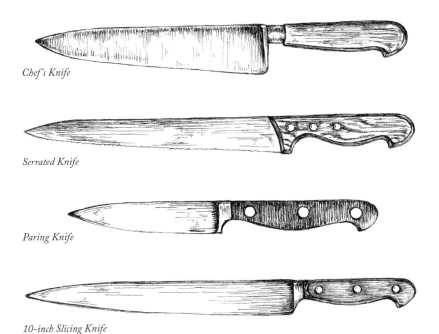

Chef's Knife

Serrated Knife

Paring Knife

10-inch Slicing Knife

knife). We don't use paring knives on a cutting board—we like them for smaller tasks and for cutting stuff out of hand, grandma-style, like slicing a peach.

If you're going to get one more, buy a **10-inch slicing knife** to round out the selection. With a long blade and a thin belly, it's an ideal knife for slicing big pieces of meat, like the rib eye on page 148 and the pork roast on page 149.

If you want your knives to stay sharp and don't have some local Geppetto who can sharpen them for you, get a **waterstone.** These are sold in different grits, much like sandpaper, and you want #1000. Soak the thing in water for a few hours before using

it. Remove the stone from the water, but keep the basin nearby. Have a rag or some paper towels on hand and a bowl of clean water when you set out to sharpen your knives. Use your fingers to flick water over the top of the stone to wet it, then, being careful to keep the knife at a steady, consistent angle (between 20 and 30 degrees to the stone) and applying a steady, even pressure along the blade, draw it back and forth across the stone. After a few passes, wipe away with the rag the slurry of grit that will have accumulated on the blade, rewet the stone, and repeat. Give each side of the knife a few passes.

And don't believe the hype that serrated knives can't be sharpened;

we do it all the time. We see serrated knives as future slicing knives that just have to be sharpened a couple hundred times and worn down.

A **clam knife** (we like the Dexter) has a flat, thin, dull blade. We've seen cooks use a sharp paring knife instead of a clam knife. To each his own, as long as you remember that the cutting board in this particular operation happens to be your hand, and if you miss your mark, well . . . it's your hand. So get a clam knife, or don't blame us.

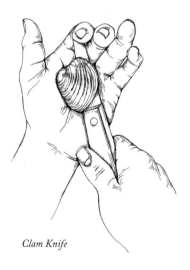

Clam Knife

LADLE & WHISK

One of each should cover it. A big ladle, one that can scoop up four ounces at a time, is a good all-purpose model. And a not-too-big, not-too-stiff, not-too-soft, and not-too-heavy whisk is ideal. It's a Goldilocks situation: you've got to try out a few at the store to see what feels right in your hand. Beyond that, buy an all-metal whisk. Wooden handles are cute but harder to wash thoroughly, and they tend to wear out before the rest of the whisk.

Ladle & Whisk

MIXING BOWLS

Stainless steel is the best. The bigger the bowls, the better, and the more, the merrier. Get a set of three or four or five nesting bowls at a kitchen-ware store and then augment them with one or two really, really big bowls—big enough to wash a baby in kind of big. They'll seem excessive until you try to make pasta and salad for too many people. Then you'll be thankful.

Stainless Steel Mixing Bowl

PALETTE KNIFE

Palette knives—the 10-inch-long models—are typically used for frosting cakes; they'll be available in the baking section of any kitchenware shop.

Back in the eighties, you couldn't find an aspiring cook in France who didn't have one—a little three- or four-inch model—in his knife kit. It was the most fashionable thing to flip a scallop with.

And we think—little or big—the thin, firm "blade" (it is dull on both sides) makes a palette knife the nicest tool for cutting gnocchi. You could use a butter knife, but we think it's worth the $3 to get one of these.

Palette Knife

PASTA MACHINE

Worth the (small) investment if you have any interest in making fresh pasta at home. Atlas is our favorite manufacturer for stainless-steel hand-cranked models, though if you have a KitchenAid stand mixer, you could opt for the motorized roller attachment they make for the machine. It's a good way to make the mixer more versatile.

Most pasta machines will come with one cutting attachment that has two settings—thin for linguine, wide for fettuccine. Start with that. If you find that you're regularly making fresh pasta, reward yourself with an additional attachment, like one for pappardelle and spaghetti.

Find instructions for how to make fresh pasta on page 94.

Pasta Machine

PEPPER MILL

Do not pass Go without two: one for black pepper, one for white pepper. They will make all the difference. Look for Peugeot pepper mills, the brand you see in every great kitchen in France (Peugeot's home turf) and

Pepper Mill

around the world. The gears of their grinders are made the same way they were when the company started out, back in 1842. Peugeot grinders finely crush the peppercorns rather than mash them like other cheaper mills made with plastic gears will do. Plastic and pepper were never meant to be friends.

POTS & PANS

There's always quality to be considered when you're talking about pots. Aluminum pots are crap. Don't buy them. Copper pots are the best if you can afford them.

Good heavy stainless steel does the trick every time. Brand-wise, we think All-Clad makes the best American pots and pans, and Sitram does a killer job if you're down with buying French. Both are expensive; if you're looking for an affordable, long-lasting, and reliable brand, track down a restaurant supply shop that stocks WinCo.

Pots & Pans

As far as which pans, you've probably got some already. You could conquer the world with two skillets, a 10-inch and a 14-inch; one 3- or 4-quart sauté pan (like a skillet but with higher straight sides); one 5-quart sautoir; and one or two stockpots. (With two you can boil water for pasta in one and make the Sunday sauce in the other.)

RECTANGULAR BAKING PAN

Get one or two: 8 by 10, 9 by 12, it doesn't really matter. For lasagna, tiramisu, etc., enameled cast iron or quality glazed ceramic is the best. Look for a pan that feels heavy for its size.

Baking Pan

SHEET PANS

Baking sheets, essentially. But you want the heavy-duty aluminum rimmed ones from the restaurant supply store. The size you're looking for is called a "half sheet pan." (Full sheet pans are too big for most

Sheet Pan

home ovens.) Use them for roasting, baking, oven browning, even storing stuff on. Sheet pans are one of the most versatile and useful items in the kitchen.

SALAD SPINNER

A no-brainer. Makes washing and drying greens—and drying the excess water off of the leaves is really the challenge—impossible to mess up. See page 66 for instructions on using it.

SCALE

Digital scales are excellent but expensive; spring-loaded scales are cheaper and better looking. Whatever kind of scale you get, make sure it will measure at least 2 pounds and has a setting that allows you to zero it. (If you do get one with springs, never pick it up by the weighing tray: that will stretch out the springs and throw off the accuracy.) Scales are indispensable for portioning pasta (fresh or dry)

Scale

and weighing ingredients that don't lend themselves to being stuffed in a cup (like the right amount of fresh bread for meatballs).

SIEVE & COLANDER

Related but different. The sieve should be fine-meshed, for straining broths, etc. Water should run freely through the colander; it's for washing fruits and vegetables and draining pasta. You need both.

Sieve

STAND MIXER

Stand mixers are expensive, they take up counter or cupboard space when not in use. It is absolutely possible to manually do every job a stand mixer can do. But the time and energy you're not expending kneading pasta—or the tennis elbow–like strain you're saving yourself from by not hand-whipping cream or egg whites—seems like one of those trade-offs that's worth a couple of weeks of instant ramen dinners. Mixers like the KitchenAid can also take on attachments like a meat grinder (for making sausage or grinding beef fresh for burgers or meatballs) that give it even more versatility. If you're deciding between a food processor, a blender, and a stand mixer for a big kitchen purchase, there's no debate: the stand mixer will save you the most time and get the most use.

KitchenAid Mixer

VEGETABLE PEELER

Falcinelli likes the old-school EKCO stainless steel swivel-blade peeler—the kind you find in every pantry and supermarket and deli or hardware store. Castronovo likes the Swiss-made Zyliss Y peeler— the stirrup-shaped model—and says that the Swiss make a better blade. Whatever kind of peeler you end up with, use it for peeling vegetables or cutting thin curls of firmer cheeses to garnish pastas and salads.

Y Peeler

PASTRY EQUIPMENT

Dessert requires its own *batterie de cuisine*. Luckily, it can be purchased piecemeal: get a tart pan when you're going to make a tart; the ramekins and torch when you're having a party and want to impress friends with the Vanilla Bean Crème Brûlée (see page 166); and so forth.

BLOWTORCH

The hardware-store variety, for making crème brûlée. (And if you're thinking, "Spend money on a blow-torch just to make crème brûlée?" you're not thinking of all the things you can light on fire with it.)

Blowtorch

BUNDT PAN

Why a Bundt pan? Because it makes a good-looking cake. Bundt pans also yield more browned surface area— call it cake crust if you like—than a regular cake pan, and we like that outer crispy part of the cake more than the spongy soft center. We use mini Bundt molds for our Olive Oil

Cake (page 177), but the recipe works just as well in one big Bundt pan.

Mini Bundt Pan

CRÈME BRÛLÉE RAMEKINS

Some stores sell 4-ounce aluminum versions, but the ceramic ones are the ticket if you really care about your crème brûlée (see the recipe on page 166.)

ROLLING PIN

A rolling pin with handles and ball bearings is the model you're looking for. Wood is the way to go—you never see those marble rolling pins from the gourmet stores in professional kitchens. In a pinch, though, you can always substitute a parchment-wrapped wine bottle.

Rolling Pin

SPRINGFORM PAN

For the Ricotta Cheesecake (page 169), go for the 9- or 10-inch version.

Springform Pan

TART PAN

For the Chocolate Tart (page 172), we use a 10-inch fluted pan with a removable bottom.

Tart Pan

PANTRY

The better the ingredients you start with, the less work you'll have to do. But it's more important to worry about freshness than "betterness." The fresher your ingredients, the fresher your food is going to taste. That oversized jar of bay leaves you bought on sale years ago? They taste like it. The prize bottle of olive oil you got as a present and are saving for the right occasion? It's getting worse by the day. It's important to go through your pantry every once in a while and clean it out. Nothing should sit around for more than a few months. (If it has, use it and then buy less of it the next time around.)

One last note: We like to store ingredients, especially things like flour and semolina, in quart Ball jars, labeled with the date and what's in them. Lined up in the pantry (and kept out of the light), they look good, and the jars and lids can be run through the dishwasher.

KITCHEN BASICS

Here are a few ingredients we assume you've got on hand:

All-Purpose Flour: We prefer organic flour, which is easier and easier to find these days. Choose flour that hasn't been bleached or bromated.

Garlic & Onions: These should be stored in the open air and in a well-ventilated place such as a wicker basket on the counter.

Butter: Buy it regularly and in small quantities—enough so you never run out but can always see the possibility just around the corner. Freshness is paramount with butter. You wouldn't drink old cream, so why would you spread it on your toast?

Sugar—Granulated & Powdered: Obvious, necessary.

ANCHOVIES & TUNA
(FISH THAT KEEP)

Sicilian fish packed in olive oil are the best. Find them at a good Italian shop.

Flott Tuna

Agostino Recca Sardines

BREAD
FRESH BREAD

Always have bread on hand and you will always have something to eat. Buy crusty country bread—with a crisp, dark crust that crackles but ultimately gives when you squeeze it, and a chewy-tender interior with an uneven crumb laced with irregular, bubbly holes.

LEFTOVER BREAD

Leftover bread is God's way of saying, "Make French toast." If you want to heed that advice, see page 192. Otherwise, do what we do with most of ours: cut the crusts off and leave those out to stale (for bread crumbs, see below); wrap up the crustless tender leftover inside stuff and freeze it. It's the perfect "fresh bread" to use in our meatball recipe (page 124).

BREAD CRUMBS

Stale crusts (see above) and bread, left out until it's crackling dry, can be ground into delicious bread crumbs in the food processor. Store the crumbs in a tightly sealed container in the freezer, and use to garnish pastas (like Linguine with Fava Beans, Garlic, Tomato & Bread Crumbs on page 106) and to lighten up Meatballs (page 124).

BROTHS & STOCKS

Homemade broths aren't something that you keep in the pantry cabinet, but everybody reading this book has a freezer, and the freezer is a great way to keep broths handy. Then, when you need broth, it's as easy as melting an ice cube on the stovetop. That said, the vegetable broth's delicacy and freshness are two of its chief attributes, so try to make it when you need it.

CHEESE BROTH

Cheese broth is one of our staple preparations, a way to squeeze the last bit of flavor out of the pounds and pounds of Pecorino Romano we go through every week. Cheese broth isn't super-flavorful on its own, but the long, slow simmering extracts the essence from the cheese. And by "essence" we mean the naturally occurring MSG that imparts flavor and savoriness.

We go through so much cheese that we can pack to the brim every pot of broth we make, but you really only need about an ounce per quart, so the rind (the dry outer half inch or so of a hard cheese) from a good-sized chunk of Pecorino Romano (or Parmesan or any grating cheese) should be sufficient. If you want to amp up the flavor, use more rind. Just combine the cheese and a quart of water and simmer over low heat for 2 hours, or for as long as you can. Strain and use, or store it—up to a week in the fridge or for months in the freezer.

VEAL STOCK

The only meat stock we use is a veal stock—and we use it only for braising, not for soups or sauces. To be completely honest, the only reason we use it is that we have a great kitchen crew, and they just don't sleep right unless there's veal stock in the house.

Years of working at French restaurants will do that to you.

The recipe, should you be the sort of home cook who doesn't feel as if she's cooking unless there's veal stock in the freezer, is on page 145. Otherwise, just add a few extra bones (veal or beef) to any of the braises in this book that call for veal stock and save yourself the trouble.

VEGETABLE BROTH

When we're not using cheese broth, vegetable broth is our broth of choice—it adds flavor and depth and roundness to a dish without making its presence emphatically known. Make it in as big or small a batch as you like, using trimmings, scraps, and peelings in addition to fresh vegetables.

We don't follow a specific recipe for our vegetable broth, it's catch as catch can: Take whatever size pot you've got, fill it with chopped carrots, onions, leeks, celery (usually celery root, because we have it left over from the Fennel, Celery Root, Parsley & Red Onion Salad with Lemon & Olive Oil, page 84), fennel, mushrooms and/or their trimmings, and parsley stems. Toss in a bay leaf and a few whole white peppercorns, cover the vegetables with water by 2 inches, and bring to a boil. Then turn the heat down to low and simmer for 15 minutes.

After that, remove the pot from the heat and let the broth steep for 30 to 45 minutes. Strain it and use it, or store it—up to a week in the fridge or for months in the freezer.

───────◦◦⊱⊰◦◦───────

CANNED TOMATOES

La Valle is our day-in, day-out brand of canned tomatoes. We use their "pomodori pelati italiani," whole peeled Italian tomatoes grown near Naples, in the Campania region of southern Italy. They're excellent, fairly priced, delicious tomatoes.

Tomatoes from that region are grown in volcanic soil that imparts a subtle but definite minerality. The variety of tomato grown in the region is dense, with thick flesh and just the right amount of seeds, and the resulting canned tomatoes cook down into a beautiful sauce. The southern Italian sunlight ripens the tomatoes fully, making them sweet. There is never a need to add a corrective pinch of sugar to a sauce made with these tomatoes.

The super premium tomatoes are labeled "DOP" and will say the words "San Marzano" on them. La Valle's are DOP Dell'agro Sarnese Nocerino, from a recognized region of the San Marzano growing area. Because of cost, they're impractical for us to cook with. We go through tons of tomatoes every year, and the regular La Valle tomatoes are great.

Bottom line: It's important to find real Italian tomatoes for our recipes. If you can afford the true San Marzanos, all the better. Inspect the can carefully if you don't know the brand, and make sure it specifies that that's where the tomatoes are from. (There's an American brand labeled "San Marzano" that notes in the tiniest type possible the fact that the tomatoes aren't Italian.) Not all canned tomatoes are created equal.

Canned Tomatoes

DRIED BEANS & OTHER LEGUMES

Dried beans and other legumes are the definition of a pantry staple. With beans and a little of just about anything else, you've got a meal.

Our go-to bean is the cannellini, or Great Northern. Lentils are next in line. When we worked in French restaurants, we had it drilled into our heads that lentils du Puy were the only way to go; when you're cooking Italian, everybody will tell you that it's all about Umbrian lentils. Let us sort it out for you: same thing, different country. Get little green lentils from wherever, and you'll be fine. In the winter, we cook gigante beans— a big, fava-sized bean of Greek descent—to serve with braised pork shanks.

The one rule we have—whether they're going into a soup or a crostini topping or a main course—is to soak dried beans for at least 8 hours before cooking them. We find it makes the beans and whatever dish they're in far more digestible.

Hellmann's is like Heinz ketchup —just one of those unique American ingredients that is irreplaceable in many recipes. Not just because Mom or Grandma or Jens at the deli used it, but because it has a specific, unique, and (we think) excellent flavor. We wouldn't use it for a special remoulade or tartar sauce where that homemade eggy flavor would serve the dish better, but for sandwiches—and our Romaine Hearts with Caesar Salad Dressing (page 76)—Hellmann's is the right choice.

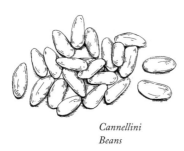

Cannellini Beans

Hellmann's Mayonnaise

HELLMANN'S MAYONNAISE (BEST FOODS MAYONNAISE IF YOU'RE OUT WEST)

Richard Hellmann, a German immigrant, owned a delicatessen in New York City at the turn of the last century, and it was from there that he built his mayonnaise fortune. As teenagers, we both worked in delis in Queens— Falcinelli in a German deli that went through 50 gallons of the stuff a week—and Hellmann's has been a staple in our refrigerators ever since.

NUTS

We keep pine nuts and walnuts on hand at all times for salads, pestos, and granola. It's advisable to buy nuts in small quantities—a pound or less at a time—and keep them out of the light. Freshness is important when it comes to nuts. To that end, once you stock up, burn through them every way you can: scatter them over your morning oatmeal or granola, serve them drizzled with honey next to cheese, and so on.

OILS & VINEGARS

Grapeseed oil is our preferred neutral cooking and salad oil. It's got a high smoke point, meaning it won't burn and break down and start smelling and tasting bad when you're cooking with it, and it has a clean flavor—with a slight, pleasant bitterness to the finish—that is great in a salad dressing. Grapeseed is more expensive than corn or canola or peanut oil, but we like it best. If you are looking for a less expensive alternative, sunflower oil would be our second choice.

Then there are the flavoring oils: walnut and pumpkinseed. You won't go through much of them, but they bring a lot to the salad game, so we buy high-quality oils in small bottles. We like French walnut oil and pumpkinseed oil from Austria. Styrian pumpkinseed oil, from Graz, the same town Arnold Schwarzenegger's from, is some of the most delicious stuff out there. Store your nut oils in the fridge to keep them from going rancid.

And though we call for only scant amounts of them, know that nut oils are great secret weapons to pull out in a pinch to drizzle over greens or raw vegetables.

OLIVE OIL

Olive oil. Green gold. We go through a shipping container's worth of the stuff every year. Turn to page 18 for the story behind ours and a few tips on how to treat olive oil at home.

VINEGARS

The vinegars we use are straightforward: **red wine** and **cider** vinegars for vinaigrettes, and **balsamic** vinegar every once in a while to sweeten things up. We like French wine vinegar, American cider vinegar (like the stuff at the health food store that's packaged with the "mother," the culture that turns vinegar into vinegar, in the bottle), and balsamic vinegar that isn't the bottom-of-the-barrel supermarket brand but isn't that $100-an-eyedropper real *aceto balsamico* either.

And while we don't cook with it, we always keep **white vinegar** on hand, at home as well as at the restaurants. We find it to be a preferable, natural alternative to bleach—great on windows and floors and food surfaces, like countertops and cutting boards. It smells way better than bleach and is better for the environment.

FRANKIES OLIVE OIL

Back in the primordial ideas-on-napkins days of planning the Spuntino, we envisioned that one day we'd start producing and selling products like olive oil and canned tomato sauce. We didn't have a plan for how that would happen exactly, and most of those ideas are still scribbled on napkins somewhere.

But thanks to this redheaded thirty-something Sicilian, our friend Tommaso Asaro, we've been importing our own label of olive oil since 2007.

Tommaso is the third generation of Asaros to run his family's olive oil business, which started out as an olive-growing operation way back in 1875.

In 1916, the Asaros opened a frantoia that was, as Tommaso puts it, "like a co-op but not a co-op." (*Frantoia* is the Italian word for the place where the olives are pressed.) Farmers from the surrounding area could have their olives pressed at the Asaros' and take the resulting oil home with them; those who had extra olives, or who wanted only the first pressing—the best oil, which they would serve to their family— would sell the Asaros their excess, and the Asaros turned around and started bottling and marketing it.

In the 1940s, one of Tommaso's uncles, Anthony Asaro, moved to New York to expand the market his family was reaching. He opened Asaro Brothers Company, or ABC, an old-school cheese and olive shop out in the back end of Bushwick, Brooklyn. We knew the place: it was a dead ringer for Genco Pura, Vito Corleone's olive oil shop in *The Godfather*. (It closed in 2006, shortly after we got to know Tommaso.) ABC supplied Asaro oils, mainly the Partanna brand, to other Italian stores in Queens and Brooklyn and helped the family make inroads here.

The business that Tommaso runs is less mom-and-pop than that: It is one of the biggest olive oil producers in Sicily. His family has accumulated a patchwork of properties planted with old-growth olive trees across western Sicily. (They started buying up the land in 1875 and continue to this day.) Today they hold the rights to land in which the roots of more than 30,000 trees grow.

Tommaso is working to modernize the business. In 2006, he converted all the land his family owns to USDA-approved organic cultiva-

tion, turning away from herbicides and pesticides. In 2008, he finished building a new frantoia, a gleaming white building on a hillside in Partanna that uses the latest technology to make olive oil. Contrary to the warm and fuzzy image of great oil coming from olives pressed in some old-school, mule-drawn stone-wheel mill, the clean, temperature-controlled modern facilities that Tommaso's family uses make for cleaner, great-tasting oils. (Grit and grime and broiling summer temperatures are not olive oil's friends.) It's clear that the locals agree: during harvest season, wizened and sunburned old men line up their tiny tractors along the road leading to the frantoia, each toting a tower of crated olives that will be custom pressed just for them.

The first fall after we met Tommaso, we traveled to Partanna to work up a profile for our oil. The first oils we got from Tommaso were on the lighter side; we were looking for more fruit and a fuller body. The second year we switched to a blend that's mostly Nocellara del Belice olives (which give the oil greenness, a core of fruity flavor, and luxurious body); a little Biancolilla for balance and sweetness; and some Cerasuola olives, which add almond, artichoke, and floral notes. The next year we arranged that all the olives would come from the family's organic DOP olive groves, and since then our oil has been 100 percent Nocellara del Belice. (The DOP, or *Denominazione di Origine Protetta,* label is assurance from the Italian government that the olives are specific varieties traditionally grown in a particular place that is recognized to have desirable qualities.) The olive trees stretch up along the gently sloping hillsides of the valley on either side of the Belice River.

The trees are believed to be between 300 and 400 years old. Sometime long ago—we've been told it was the sixteenth century, but nobody knows for sure—the people who tended the hills blanketed the land with flat, smooth, oval stones hauled up from the riverbed. The stones help cool the ground and store moisture in the soil in the sun-scorched valley. The trees are hand-pruned, and the olives are handpicked. All those details, married to the sunlight spectrum of Sicily, matched with the volcanic soil, and influenced by the constant saline breeze from the Mediterranean, combine to make the oils from Tommaso's family so versatile and special.

While we're totally committed to these Sicilian oils—particularly ours—let us recommend a couple of ground rules for the use of olive oil:

* "Cold-pressed extra-virgin" olive oil is the only olive oil to spend your money on. Cold-pressed extra-virgin is, essentially, the purest olive oil—the first oil that gushes out of just-picked and gently pressed fruit. Use it for everything.

* Avoid heating olive oil to the point where it smokes. It kills the flavor and makes it harder to digest—or harder on the stomach, anyway.

* Olive oil doesn't improve with age. Buy what you need and use what you do buy quickly. Do not hoard oil or save it for special occasions; do not have six half-used bottles that linger in a cabinet for months on end. Buy the best you can, drain it, and replace it.

* There are plenty of nonculinary uses for olive oil. We've had bartenders who soaked their fingertips in it to protect their cuticles from the night's wear and tear; girl-friends who've rubbed it into their scalps, keeping it there for a half hour to get a lustrous shine. Also it's an effective, if expensive, mois-turizer for chapped hands in the wintertime.

———∽o◯∼o◦———

OLIVES

We use three kinds of olives, all Italian, at Frankies. While there is a time and place and purpose for canned olives (camping), we vastly prefer to buy them in brine in bulk from a conscientious importer or specialty shop.

Castelvetrano and Nocellara del Belice are the olives of choice in the area of Sicily where our olive oil comes from, and we love them for their bright, sunshiney flavor and meaty texture. The Gaeta is a common Mediterranean olive, most often encountered as a medium-sized black olive from Greece; we get big green Gaetas from Lazio, near Rome, that are super-meaty.

Good Italian delis—places with big wheels of Parmigiano-Reggiano out on their marble counters and the family running the show—are going to carry these olives or olives of a similar character and quality. Upscale shops and gourmet supermarkets are another solid bet.

Regardless of the variety or place of origin, the particulars of the olives in front of you are what is important. They should be fruity, slightly bitter, and neither super-soft (though some-times good, tiny niçoise olives are quite soft) nor too firm. To make it simpler: when you can't stop eating them, that's when you know they're good olives.

See page 28 for how we dress up olives.

PASTA (DRIED)

At the Spuntino, we cook with fresh pasta, but we would never be caught without dried pasta in our pantry. If you have dried pasta and just about anything else in your kitchen, you're not too far away from having something to eat. Italian brands like Barilla and De Cecco use a qual-ity of flour superior to the typical

American supermarket brands. See the chapter starting on page 89 for more thoughts on pasta.

SEASONINGS
PEPPER

We use white pepper for cooking just about everything. If we could only have one pepper on hand, it would be white pepper, without question. It's a hang-up that we picked up working in French kitchens and have never let go of. White pepper is elegant. It's aromatic. It's a big part of the flavor of our food. The funkier, more complex, more nuanced flavor of white pepper can stand up to cooking, and it doesn't speckle a dish the way black pepper does.

There's something in the affinity and interplay of Pecorino Romano—our cooking cheese of choice—and white pepper that just knocks it out of the park. Maybe nobody would ever guess that this is the secret flavor combination behind a lot of our dishes, but there you go.

In our kitchens, black pepper is a finishing pepper, something to add right at the end. The flavor of black pepper is best when it is ground as freshly as possible. The power of the pepper dissipates in long cooking, and pregrinding deadens it. So we usually add black pepper by grinding it over a finished dish right at the table.

A couple of things: Fresh peppercorns are worth seeking out. If the selection at your supermarket is dusty, look elsewhere or online. Don't buy in bulk unless you're going to churn through pepper. And no preground pepper products: think of them as related to but not the real thing. You can get decent pepper grinders for not too much cash, and you'll never regret the investment.

SEA SALT

All salt called for in this book (unless otherwise specified) is fine sea salt. We believe that all salt is not created equal and that sea salt is the best salt for cooking and eating. We prefer the idea of salt foraged from the seas to the thought of all the mining and refining that goes into kosher and table salt.

SPICES

The typical Italian-American kitchen is all about oregano. We barely ever use it. In fact, other than pepper, we prefer to rely on fresh seasonings—**garlic, parsley** (lots of parsley), **sage,** and so on—for most of our savory cooking. We throw **bay leaves** into our non-tomato meat braises, because who doesn't? There's one dirty little secret in our pantry: **Chinese five-spice powder,** something Castronovo started cooking with after working in Hong Kong. (Long story.) Used in tiny, tiny amounts—so little you can barely detect it—it supercharges the flavor of sweet potatoes and squash. **Vanilla beans** and **cloves** and **cinnamon sticks** go into the desserts.

SEMOLINA

We use coarse-ground semolina flour to make our polenta. (Most polenta is made with cornmeal.) Semolina is a derivative of durum wheat, the same kind used to make dried pasta and the same stuff used to make Cream of Wheat. Buy it in small bags and store it out of the light. If you can't find coarsely ground semolina, you can always swap out cornmeal for our polenta, though the resulting mush will be less smooth and creamy.

FRESH HERBS TO KEEP ON HAND

Okay, fresh herbs aren't a "pantry" item exactly, but they are something that can be turned to in a pinch to brighten up nearly any dish.

Parsley is the herb we use more than anything else. Keep it fresh by wrapping it in a damp paper towel. This works for **mint** and **basil,** too, though if you buy a bunch of basil with roots still attached, you can try standing it up in a pint glass of water instead. It should keep for a couple of days.

Rosemary, sage, and **thyme** keep well in a breathable but enclosed container—like a plastic bag with a few holes in it. Keep them dry. As with all herbs, water reduces their shelf life, so wash them just before putting them to use.

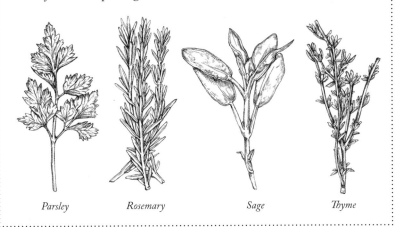

Parsley   *Rosemary*   *Sage*   *Thyme*

CHAPTER 2

ANTIPASTO

The concept of antipasto is integral to the Spuntino way of eating. To us it means a substantial and delicious variety of tastes that are used to jump-start a meal—or, if you really do it up right, it can be a meal in itself.

A spread of meats and cheeses and olives, maybe a vegetable, and some olive oil and bread—that's the way to feed people. If you start off a dinner with a plated appetizer and then move on to a plated entrée, the vibe is "This is mine; that is yours." A generous spread of antipasto plopped down in the middle of the table, spilling over the edges of a wooden cutting board or sprawling across big platters, says, "Hey, everybody, dig in." It says it's family-style, communal, that it's a meal to be shared, one that everybody is eating together, not separately. When you start out sharing, that feeling of conviviality continues throughout the meal—passing plates, talking about what you're eating—and will make for a better night. It's the right way to kick things off.

And it's not just some Italian *abbondanza* thing: get a group together for a meal, and everybody's going to come in on their own trip. Somebody ate a burger for lunch and isn't hungry. Somebody's on a diet. Somebody's ravenous. An antipasto spread lets everybody glide into dinner at their own pace, eating as much or as little as they want.

Another good thing about antipasto: a lot of the work gets done when you shop for dinner. Find a place you trust with meats and cheeses you like and you know are of good quality, and you're halfway there.

Antipasto can be practically anything Italian that's served at room temperature—meats, cheeses, vegetables, crostini, jarred artichoke hearts, whatever. The important thing is the variety.

Here's how we do it.

AN ANTIPASTO PLATE AT THE SPUNTINO

CHEESE ───────────────

Unleashing a little cheese for your
friends or family to nibble on before
the meal is always a good idea. It'll buy
you extra time to get done whatever
you forgot to do before they remember
they're hungry. See pages 32–33 for ideas
about selecting and serving it.

CURED MEATS ──────

Cured meat—or, in
Italian, salumi—is salty,
and salt gets the juices
going, prompts the body,
and gets you hungry. We
serve a minimum of two
cured meats as part of an
antipasto platter—a whole-
muscle meat, like prosciutto
or capicola, and a chopped
meat, like soppressata or
cacciatorini. See pages
29–31 for more info.

ON THE SIDE: BREAD & OIL

Good bread and fresh extra virgin olive oil
are imperative. They round out the antipasto
selection and anchor the meal. Look for an
olive oil that's so delicious you would drink it
straight from the bottle.

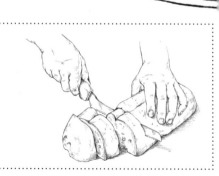

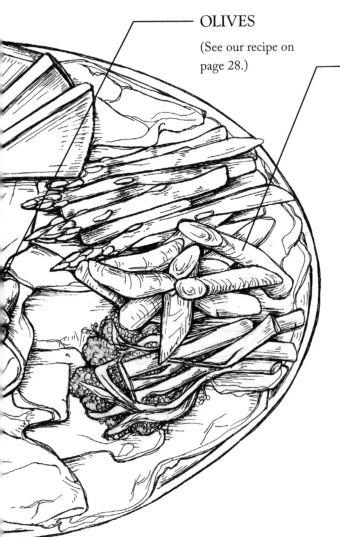

OLIVES

(See our recipe on
page 28.)

VEGETABLES

The more traditional
Italian or Italian-
American approach to
vegetables as part of an
antipasto spread would
be artichokes in oil or
pickled mushrooms or
any of those prepared
vegetables you probably
know from your Italian
deli. We love that stuff,
too. But as a way to
alleviate the onslaught
of salt and add some
balance—and, yes, even
a little healthfulness—
we serve very simply
cooked and lightly
seasoned vegetables as
part of our antipasto
spread at the Spuntino.
See pages 34–45 for
recipes.

CROSTINI

Crostini are the extra-credit work of the antipasto hour, though by no means
necessary. You can—as we do—make easy work of them by using ingredients
you're preparing for other dishes or meals. Crostini are, quite simply, delicious
eats on toast. But they are delicious eats on toast that your guests will be
disproportionately excited about. Recipes start on page 46.

OLIVES

Olives round out the antipasto spread. To make a quart of our marinated olives, get your hands on 2 pints (4 cups) of olives, preferably a mix of Castelvetrano, Nocellara del Belice, and Gaeta. Drain them in a strainer in the sink and give them a quick rinse under the faucet. Transfer them to a small bowl, one that accommodates them snugly and is made of a nonreactive material like stainless steel or ceramic. While you're packing them in there, add seasonings: a sprig of fresh rosemary, 2 cloves of roughly chopped garlic, and the zest of 1 lemon, removed with a vegetable peeler. Top with good olive oil—you'll need as much as 2 cups. They will keep for a week or so in the refrigerator; make sure to let them warm up to room temperature and remove them from the oil before serving.

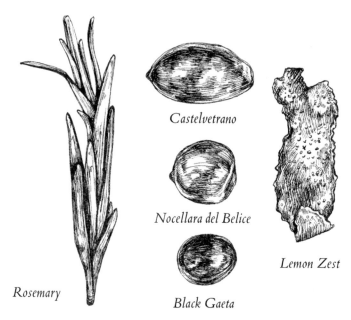

Castelvetrano

Nocellara del Belice

Lemon Zest

Rosemary

Black Gaeta

WORK CLEAN

When making this kind of prepare-and-store dish, always work with clean hands, a clean board, clean ingredients, and clean containers to keep spoilage and contamination at bay.

CURED MEATS

In general, we figure on about 2 ounces per person for prosciutto or another meat in that family and a little less for the chopped-meat salami-type items. That said, Big Frank, Falcinelli's dad, can eat half a pig's leg in a single sitting, so it's always good to lay in some extra supplies.

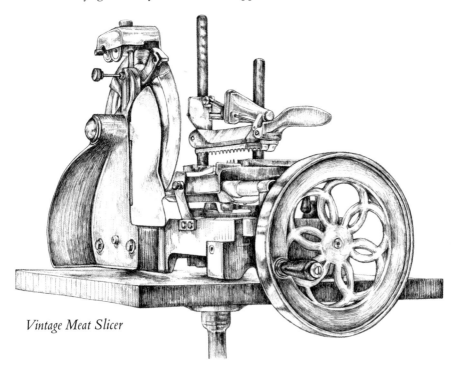

Vintage Meat Slicer

"WHOLE-MUSCLE" CURED MEATS"

Prosciutto, the leg of the pig, is the king of the whole-muscle cured meats. Our everyday prosciutto is one from Parma, aged for about 12 months, the kind of prosciutto you'd find at any respectable Italian deli. If you want to get fancier, try out a longer-aged ham when they've got it

on offer, or a prosciutto from a different part of Italy (San Daniele hams, from the northeast, are sweeter and more buttery) or a domestic prosciutto from a high-quality producer, like La Quercia Rosso, out of Iowa.

Speck is like prosciutto, except that it's not aged as long and, most importantly, it's smoked. The style developed up in the alpine reaches of Italy, where it gets cold and snowy during the winter. The story goes that after the November slaughter, families used to hang their hams up to cure inside the tops of their chimneys, where it was warm enough that the hams wouldn't freeze during the early months of the year. The process imparted a smoky flavor to the hams, and speck was born. It's a nice change of pace from prosciutto.

And then there's **capicola,** or as the people we grew up around called it, "gabbagool." Capicola is boned pork shoulder that's been seasoned and cured, then rolled up tight and stuffed into a wide casing and hung to age. (Capicola looks like a salami/sausage, but when you cut into it, the cross section reveals it to be a whole-muscle meat.) Capicola is either spicy, which means it's been dusted with

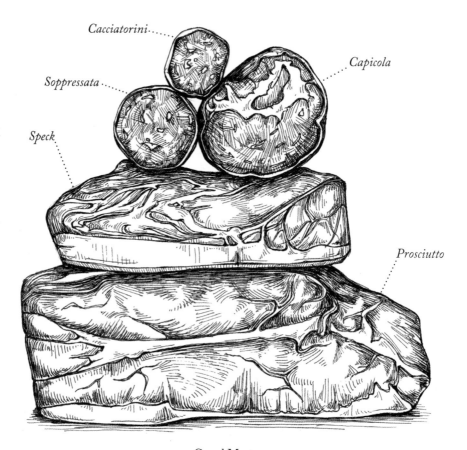

Cured Meats

red pepper, or sweet, which means it's been cured with just the traditional garlic, black pepper, and Italian spices.

Assuming that you don't have a Berkel meat slicer, enough room in your fridge for a pig's leg, and a brood that can eat its way through a whole cured pork shoulder before it starts to dry out (which is surprisingly fast once you cut into it), your best bet is buying whole-muscle meats sliced to order at the deli. Properly sliced, layered on wax-coated paper, and tightly wrapped—the way any deli worth a damn will sell them—the meat will keep perfectly for the first 24 hours and then start to go downhill after that.

"GROUND MEAT" CURED MEATS

The salamis in salumi are all variations on a theme. The proportion of fat to lean changes, as does the fineness of the grind of the meat, the seasonings, the girth and length (both of which depend on the kind of animal's intestines the sausage is stuffed into), the length of the cure, etc. When you're shopping for these kinds of cured meats, look for the meat to be a deep purple or crimson interspersed with lily-white fat. Browning meat or yellow fat are both bad, or at least not encouraging signs.

Our favorites are **cacciatorini,** which are typically the smallest dry-cured sausages you're going to find, an inch or less in diameter and short enough to stick in your pocket and take out into the woods on a boar hunt. (*Caccia* means hunter.) Cacciatorini are most often made with finely ground meat and mildly spiced; they shouldn't be aged so long that they're rock hard, though we do like them on the firmer, drier side. Even if you're not hunting wild pigs, they're a good choice for picnics or fishing trips. (Just remember to bring a knife along to slice them.)

The other ground-meat cured meat we serve (and eat pounds and pounds of) is spicy and sweet **soppressata.** Soppressata is thicker and longer than cacciatorini. It's firm and salty, the ideal "salami" to us. It's aged long enough to have a good sharpness and seasoned so there's a peppery kick on top of the pig-and-salt thing. The sweet version uses black pepper while the spicy soppressata is made with red pepper.

Buy sausages like this whole (in the case of cacciatorini) or half (soppressata) and slice them at home as you need them.

CHEESE

You can approach a cheese selection for an antipasto layout a million different ways: geographically (see our cheese map on page 207), by firmness, by relative stinkiness, or by the types of animal the milk came from. Turn to our extensive cheese guide (starting on page 202) for specifics on the cheeses we serve at the restaurant. In terms of presentation here are a few ways to go:

* **A solo show for a rock-star cheese.** Some cheeses do best standing alone, on their own little plate, in their own little spotlight. Fresh cheeses like real Neapolitan buffalo mozzarella, burrata, and stracciatella are our favorite cheeses to present this way. And the really funky, strongly flavored, super-distinctive Italian cheeses like Taleggio and Gorgonzola have strong enough personalities not to need a supporting cast.

  Parmigiano-Reggiano and provolone are everyday cheeses, but they warrant the spotlight, too. Put out a mountain of provolone at your next party and watch it get destroyed if you don't believe us.

  The important thing when you're offering one cheese or setting off one of your cheeses like this is to be generous: use whole lobes of mozzarella or burrata; pile up a mountain of Parmigiano or provolone cut into chunks; put out pieces of the smellier cheeses that are big enough to stink up the whole room. Put a couple of knives near the cheese and have plenty of bread on hand.

* **A variety show.** This is the most common approach to putting together a cheese plate at home. We're behind it, with a few caveats: Do not serve a bunch of cheeses that are similar to one another.

Do not serve more than three or four cheeses. Make sure to present cheeses in decent-sized pieces—you don't need whole wheels, but little ¼-pound nubbins are going to be all rind and quick to dry out.

So maybe serve one cow's milk cheese along with a goat's milk and a sheep's milk. Mix up the textures and the ages. A mix of aged provolone, Pecorino di Fossa, and Amalattea works for us. As an alternative, serve three cow's milk cheeses that show range—a tangy and soft three-month-old Castelrosso, a buttery and firm year-old Montasio, and a stinky-soft piece of assertive Gorgonzola.

* **Support the main act.** When we serve soft fresh cheeses, like burrata, mozzarella, etc., we find that olive oil and (maybe) black pepper are the only fancying up they need. With saltier, firmer cheeses, we usually serve a little pile of walnuts drizzled with some nice wildflower honey on the side. The sweetness and crunch break it up and provide a nice contrast to the cheese.

VEGETABLE ANTIPASTI

At the Spuntino, simply prepared vegetables are a cornerstone of our way of cooking. We mainly serve them roasted, as described here, and then repurpose them in countless ways: The sweet potatoes get mashed into a filling for ravioli (page 110) and a topping for crostini (page 49); the cauliflower replaces sausage in a vegetarian version of our cavatelli with brown butter. A mix of all these antipasto vegetables plus a little dressing become our Roasted Vegetable Salad (page 72) and the Roasted Vegetable Sandwich (page 57), and all work well as side dishes (aka contorni).

A couple more things: We don't serve any of these vegetables hot (except the Brussels sprouts, which get soggy when they cool), because they're best at room temperature or, in the case of the beets, even lightly chilled. And we don't dress or otherwise flavor our vegetable antipasti (with the exception of adding garlic to the string beans and the broccoli rabe) because we like them plain, tasting of themselves and nothing more. It's an approach rooted more in our shared interest in healthy eating than in any particular Italian ideology.

All the recipes in this section are easily and fruitfully multiplied. See the chart to make the math easy.

ROASTING TIP

When roasting carrots or cauliflower—or really any vegetable—it's important to slick the outside of the vegetables with a thin coat of oil. Why? If you don't, the surface is going to stay at right around 212°F, which is the evaporation point for water, and the vegetables will go limp before they get browned. But when you coat what you're roasting with fat or oil, the exterior can reach the temperature you set the oven to, because the oil will heat up to that temperature despite the water in the vegetable. This is important because it's the only way to ensure that the proper development of sugars is taking place as a vegetable browns.

QUICK GUIDE TO ROASTING VEGETABLES

ROAST:	AT 350°F FOR:	READY WHEN:
BEETS	1½ hours	*Yields easily to the blade of a knife, still a little bit firm.*
BRUSSELS SPROUTS	25 minutes	*Browned and crisp outside; tender and giving when squeezed.*
CARROTS	45 minutes	*Offers no resistance to the tines of a fork.*
CAULIFLOWER	40 to 50 minutes	*Mottled and brown; should have a crisp/tender chew to it, like popcorn.*
CREMINI MUSHROOMS	25 to 30 minutes	*Browned and shrunken outside; juicy inside.*
JERUSALEM ARTICHOKES	25 to 30 minutes	*Yields to the blade of a knife, but still somewhat crisp.*
SWEET POTATOES	45 minutes	*Offers no resistance to the tines of a fork; should squish if squeezed.*

ASPARAGUS

Asparagus grows in North America starting in the spring and the early summer. Buy it and cook it in season. Avoid the pallid, tough stuff sold in supermarkets the rest of the year.

1 bunch of asparagus will serve 3 or 4

Asparagus

Fine sea salt

Olive oil

1. Trim the woody bottoms of the asparagus stalks—cut off from 1 to 1½ inches. For all but the skinniest asparagus, use a vegetable peeler to peel away the fibrous outer layer from the bottom half of the stalks.

2. Bring a large pot of water to a boil and salt it well. Get out a large bowl and fill it with ice and water.

3. When the pot is boiling furiously, drop in the asparagus and cook for 2 to 3 minutes, just until they're past that raw, crunchy stage. Don't be a clock watcher: Snagging one out of the pot and eating it will tell you when the asparagus is ready.

4. Using a slotted spoon, transfer the blanched asparagus to the ice bath. Shock them in that until they've cooled and lost the heat of the pot, then transfer them to a paper-towel-lined baking sheet to drain. Arrange the asparagus on a platter, all facing the same way, and dress with a pinch of salt and a generous drizzle of olive oil.

BEETS

We use standard-sized red beets for consistency. Buy any variety you like—candy cane, golden, whatever—in any size you like and use as directed in this recipe. Smaller beets will cook a bit more quickly; check them after 45 minutes.

1. Trim off the leafy tops and scrub the beets well. Leave the skins on.

2. Heat the oven to 350°F. Line a small roasting pan with foil (to make cleanup much easier) and nestle the beets in it. Drizzle with olive oil, enough to coat them lightly, and season them generously with salt and white pepper.

3. Add a splash of water to the pan and cover it with foil.

4. Bake the beets for 1½ hours, at which point they should offer absolutely no resistance to the tip of a knife. Remove them from the oven, remove the foil from the pan, and let the beets cool slightly.

5. When they're cool enough to handle but still warm, use a kitchen towel (or your hands—either will end up dyed electric red) to rub the skin off the beets. It should come away easily. To serve the beets as an antipasto/contorni, cut them into wedges. (If you roasted them for one of the salads or sandwiches, cut into ½-inch dice.) Serve at room temperature or lightly chilled. Dress with olive oil, a pinch of salt, and a few turns of black pepper just before serving.

Each baseball-sized beet will serve 2

Beets

Olive oil

Salt and white pepper

Black pepper

BROCCOLI RABE

1 bunch of broccoli rabe will serve 2 or 3

Broccoli rabe

Olive oil

2 cloves garlic, peeled

Crushed red pepper flakes

Salt and white pepper

Some rabe is tender and some is tough, with stalks like tree saplings and leaves like sail canvas. If you can only get the latter, add a splash of water in Step 3 and let the greens cook covered for a couple of extra minutes. Repeat until tender.

1. Trim off the woody ends of the stalks and wash the broccoli rabe in a colander under running water. Give it a brief shake to lose some of the moisture, but don't out-and-out dry it off. The water clinging to the rabe will help it cook.

2. Heat ¼ cup olive oil in an 8-inch sauté pan over low heat. After a minute, add the garlic and cook it slowly for 8 to 10 minutes, until it has gone a pale gold and is sweetly aromatic, maybe starting to brown the tiniest bit around the edges.

3. When the garlic is good to go, turn the heat to medium-high and add a pinch of red pepper flakes. Cook for 30 seconds, then add the broccoli rabe, piling it as high as it needs to go. Add a large pinch of salt and a few turns of white pepper and toss to coat the rabe in the oil. Cover the pan and cook for 4 minutes.

4. Remove the lid and toss the rabe again. It should be wilted and greener than it was when it started, and the water and oil should have melded together into a nice, juicy pan sauce. Taste a piece—it should still be toothsome (al dente, in other words) but not stiff or too bitter. If it is, give it another couple of minutes. When it's ready, remove it to a platter, along with the juices from the pan, and let it cool before serving.

BRUSSELS SPROUTS

We love room temperature or chilled vegetables for an antipasto plate, but roasted Brussels sprouts get soggy and cabbagey when they cool down. You have about one hour to serve them after they come out of the oven.

1 pint of Brussels sprouts will serve 2 or 3

Brussels sprouts

Olive oil

Salt and white pepper

1. Put the Brussels sprouts in a colander and rinse them under running water. Shake them dry, then pull off and discard any loose or discolored outer leaves. Transfer them to a cutting board, trim off their stems, and cut them in half through the core.

2. Heat the oven to 350°F. Put the Brussels sprouts in a large mixing bowl, hit them with a splash of olive oil—enough to coat them lightly—and toss. Season with a large pinch of salt and a few turns of white pepper and toss again. Spread the Brussels sprouts out, cut side down, on a baking sheet with a little space between them and pop them into the oven. Roast for about 25 minutes, by which point they should be starting to brown and crisp around the edges.

3. Serve hot or warm.

CARROTS

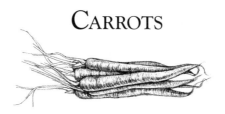

Use bunch carrots, small carrots that come with the greens attached, not those baseball-bat-sized supermarket horse carrots. Bunch carrots are sweeter, carrotier, and better eating.

A small bunch of carrots will serve 2 or 3

Carrots

Olive oil

Salt and white pepper

1. Trim the greens (leave ¼ inch attached at the top if you like) and scrub the carrots well. With smaller carrots—under ½ inch or so in diameter—there's no need to peel them. If you have any doubt, bite into one and decide for yourself whether they need to be peeled.

2. Heat the oven to 350°F. Arrange the carrots on a baking sheet—they shouldn't be crowded— and dress them with a slick of olive oil, a large pinch of salt, and a few turns of white pepper.

3. Pop the pan into the oven and roast the carrots for 40 to 45 minutes, until they are tender and their extremities are gently caramelized. Let cool. Serve at room temperature, whole or cut into halves or thirds, depending on your sensibilities and your guests.

CAULIFLOWER

1. Rip off and discard any green leaves from the cauliflower. Cut out the core and trim off any brown spots. Chop into half-dollar-sized florets.

2. Heat the oven to 350°F. Put the chopped cauliflower in a large mixing bowl and toss with a big splash of olive oil, making sure that the cauliflower is evenly and generously coated. Season with a large pinch of salt and a few turns of white pepper and toss again.

3. Spread the florets out on a baking sheet with a little space between them and pop them into the oven.

4. Roast for 40 to 50 minutes, until the florets are deeply browned and shrunken. Eight cups of raw florets (about what the average head yields) will shrink down to 2 cups during roasting. Serve warm or at room temperature, seasoned with additional salt, white pepper, and olive oil.

A medium head of cauliflower will serve 2 to 4

Cauliflower

Olive oil

Salt and white pepper

We use this roasted cauliflower in place of sausage to make a vegetarian version of the Cavatelli with Sausage & Browned Sage Butter (page 102). No reason you can't do the same.

CREMINI MUSHROOMS

Creminis are baby portobello mushrooms, like button mushrooms with dusty-brown caps. If you can't find them, substitute button mushrooms. After half an hour in a hot oven, the difference in flavor between the two isn't so great.

An 8-ounce package of cremini mushrooms will serve 2

Cremini mushrooms

Olive oil

Salt and white pepper

1. Trim off the bottoms of the mushroom stems; remove and discard any stems that seem fibrous or dried out. Brush off any clods of dirt clinging to the mushrooms. Wash the mushrooms under running water and shake them dry in a colander (or rub them in a kitchen towel until dryish—don't worry too much about the water).

2. Heat the oven to 350°F. Arrange the mushrooms in an even, well-spaced layer on a baking sheet. Dress them with olive oil (to coat evenly, lightly, etc.), a large pinch of salt, and a few turns of white pepper.

3. Pop them into the oven and roast for 25 to 30 minutes, until they're browned and shrunken and caramelized. (If you're cooking more than 1 package of mushrooms, pull the pan from the oven at the 15-minute mark and carefully tilt it to pour off the liquid the mushrooms have exuded.) Serve warm or at room temperature. Dress with an extremely generous amount of olive oil and a goodly pinch of salt.

JERUSALEM ARTICHOKES

A Jerusalem artichoke is more aptly, if less commonly, called a sunchoke, which sounds less like a thistle from Israel and more like "a bulbous tuberlike thing from the dirt end of a sunflower plant," which is what it is. They've got a sweet, earthy flavor that's great roasted, as in this recipe, or raw, shaved into a mixed salad.

1 pound of Jerusalem artichokes will serve 3 or 4

1. Scrub well: Jerusalem artichokes usually need it—but there's no need to peel them.

2. Heat the oven to 350°F. Arrange the Jerusalem artichokes in an even layer on a baking sheet. Coat them with a thin film of olive oil, sprinkle them with a big pinch of salt and a few turns of white pepper, and pop them into the oven.

3. Roast for 25 to 30 minutes, until they offer no resistance to the tip of a knife. Serve whole, warm or at room temperature. They're also good chilled and sliced into ⅛-inch-thick coins.

Jerusalem artichokes

Olive oil

Salt and white pepper

STRING BEANS

1 pound of beans serves 4 (makes 2 generous cups)

Olive oil

2 cloves garlic, peeled

Salt

Green beans, or haricots verts, if that's your thing, ends trimmed

1. Heat ¼ cup olive oil in an 8-inch sauté pan over low heat. After a minute, add the garlic and cook it slowly for 8 to 10 minutes, until it has gone a pale gold and is sweetly aromatic, maybe starting to brown the tiniest bit around the edges. Pull the pan from the heat.

2. Bring a large pot of water to a boil and salt it well. When the pot is boiling furiously, drop in the beans and cook them for 3 to 4 minutes, just until they're past that raw, crunchy stage. (Snagging one out of the pot and eating it will tell you when they're ready.)

3. Transfer the beans to a platter, sprinkle with salt, and toss them with the oil and garlic. Allow to cool to room temperature before serving.

Sweet Potatoes

1. Scrub the potatoes clean with a brush and towel them dry.

2. Heat the oven to 350°F. Slick the potatoes so their skins are covered in a thin film of olive oil. Season each potato with a pinch of salt and a few turns of white pepper, and wrap it in aluminum foil.

3. Arrange the silver-jacketed potatoes on a baking sheet with at least an inch of space between them and pop into the oven.

4. After 30 to 35 minutes, the potatoes should be a little bit tender—easily pierced with the blade of a sharp knife. If they're still tough, give them another 10 minutes, then repeat the knife test.

5. To serve, cut the potatoes into ½-inch-thick wedges or slice lengthwise into 6 steak fry–like spears.

3 good-sized sweet potatoes will serve 4

Sweet potatoes

Olive oil

Salt and white pepper

Roast a few extra sweet potatoes, and you'll have a lot of the legwork for making our ravioli (page 110) done in advance. Sweet potatoes roasted for ravioli filling can be cooked up to a couple of days in advance.

CROSTINI

What are crostini? Pieces of toast with something tasty on top—and a perfect vehicle for leftovers. Making crostini gives us new ways to use ingredients we have on hand and our customers another way to build a meal. Some nights you don't want pasta or a plate of meatballs. A few Cannellini, Caper, Lemon & Anchovy Crostini (page 49) and a hearty escarole salad will do just fine.

That's the spirit with which to approach them at home—as a way to easily and kind of elegantly round out a dinner. Toppings can be as simple as a dollop of good ricotta or a fan of ripe avocado slices. The Parsley Pesto (page 48) we use to paint our crostini toasts is about as easy to make as it gets. It shouldn't take 10 minutes to put together, and it will keep in the fridge for a week.

TOASTS FOR CROSTINI

Get a good, airy baguette or the Italian version known as a stirato and have a container of Parsley Pesto (page 48) ready.

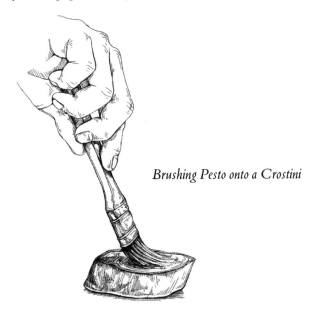

Brushing Pesto onto a Crostini

1. Cut the baguette into ¾-inch-thick slices on the bias—an angle of 30 degrees or so—which maximizes the surface area of the sliced bread. Use a brush (or, failing that, the back of a spoon) to dress both sides of each slice with parsley pesto—enough to stain the bread green, but not enough to soak it. (If you want to complete as much of the crostini making process ahead of time as possible, you can paint the bread with pesto a few hours before grilling or griddling or toasting it to order.)

2. If you're equipped for it, toast the bread in a panini press (or that George Foreman grill that you bought during a late night in front of the television) until it's crisp—about 2 minutes. No panini press? No problem. Pop the bread into a toaster oven set at high heat for about 3 minutes, until toasted, crusty, and warmed through.

3. Top the toasts with any of the toppings on the following pages while the bread is still a little bit warm, and serve.

PARSLEY PESTO

Makes a little more than 1 cup, enough for a loaf's worth of crostini

1 cup flat-leaf parsley leaves (from 1 bunch of parsley)

2 cloves garlic

1 cup olive oil

Large pinch of fine sea salt

6 to 8 turns white pepper

We brush the sliced bread for all our crostini with this pesto before toasting it.

───────⊸०⟨⟩०⊸───────

Combine all the ingredients in a blender and puree for a couple of minutes, until the mixture is an even green and smooth. Taste and adjust the salt or pepper to your liking. Store the pesto in a covered container in the refrigerator for up to a week. Shake well before using.

CANNELLINI, CAPER, LEMON & ANCHOVY

Combine all the ingredients in a small mixing bowl and stir to mix. Use at once (we put a heaping tablespoon on each crostini toast) or store in a sealed container in the refrigerator for up to a few days.

———————

That's how we make it at the restaurant. For the raid-the-cupboard version, combine: 1 cup canned cannellini beans, drained; 1 anchovy and 1 teaspoon capers, mashed or chopped together; 2 tablespoons finely chopped flat-leaf parsley; ½ teaspoon fine sea salt; ¼ teaspoon white pepper; 1 tablespoon olive oil; juice of ¼ lemon. Adjust seasoning to taste.

Enough for about 8 crostini

1 cup cooked cannellini beans (see page 60) or canned

2 tablespoons finely chopped flat-leaf parsley

½ teaspoon fine sea salt

¼ teaspoon freshly ground white pepper

1 tablespoon Parsley Pesto (opposite)

1 teaspoon Puntarelle Dressing (page 80)

SWEET POTATO

Scoop the flesh out of the potato skin and mash it in a bowl, drizzling in enough olive oil to make the mash creamy and nearly loose—maybe 2 to 3 tablespoons per potato. Season the mash with salt and white pepper. When you serve, mound 1½ tablespoons mash on each toast and drizzle with olive oil.

Enough for 6 to 8 crostini

1 sweet potato, roasted (see page 45)

Olive oil

Fine sea salt and freshly ground white pepper

AVOCADO

Enough for 4 crostini

1 Hass avocado

Olive oil

Fine sea salt and freshly ground black pepper

1. Halve the avocado: Run a knife lengthwise all the way around it, then twist it to separate the two halves. With the blade of the knife, lightly hack into the pit stuck in one of the halves, then twist the knife and pull out the pit. Slide a spoon down the side of each avocado half, between the flesh and the skin, and trace the contour and shape of the fruit to free the flesh from the skin.

2. Now you've got a couple of options. The pretty way: Cut the avocado halves lengthwise in half, then cut them lengthwise into long, slender slices. Fan them on top of the prepared toasts. The easier-to-eat way: Cut each avocado half lengthwise in half, then make 4 or 5 crosswise cuts through the quartered avocado. Arrange the chunks of avocado on top of the toasts (prepared for crostini, as directed on page 46) and serve.

RICOTTA

1. Find the best ricotta you can. Freshly made stuff from an Italian deli is your best bet. Heap it on the crostini toasts—1 generous tablespoon per toast works for us—then hit each one with a pinch of salt, a drizzle of olive oil, and a few turns of black pepper.

2. Optional but nice: We like to scatter a couple of pieces of provolone cut into matchsticks on top of the ricotta to finish. Do as you will.

Enough for about 8 crostini

1 cup fresh ricotta

Fine sea salt

Olive oil

Freshly ground black pepper

ROASTED EGGPLANT

Enough for 8 crostini

1 eggplant

2 tablespoons olive oil

½ teaspoon fine sea salt

White pepper

Freshly ground black pepper

We like this simple and direct presentation of eggplant flavor, which is about half the way to baba ghanouj. (Add some tahini, lemon, and garlic, and you're there.)

⸻

1. Heat the oven to 400°F. Slick the skin of the eggplant with the olive oil and sprinkle with the salt and white pepper. Put it on a baking sheet and put the pan in the oven. Bake for 45 minutes or an hour, until the skin is blistered in spots and a poke tells you that the insides are collapsing-soft and tender. (It's almost impossible to overcook the eggplant for this.)

2. Remove the baking sheet from the oven and let the eggplant cool for 5 to 10 minutes, so it's easier to handle.

3. Transfer the eggplant to a cutting board, slice it in half lengthwise, and use a spoon to scoop the creamy innards into a mixing bowl. Add the olive oil, salt, and white pepper to the eggplant mush, stir well to combine, and taste. Add more salt, pepper, and/or oil to the mix if necessary. You can use the eggplant at this point or store it in the refrigerator for a few days.

4. We use a generous tablespoon of eggplant on each crostini and garnish it with a drizzle of olive oil, a sprinkle of salt, and a few turns of black pepper.

CREMINI MUSHROOM & TRUFFLE OIL

Stir together all the ingredients in a mixing bowl. Taste and adjust as you like. We heap a generous tablespoon onto each crostini toast, then top each one with a teaspoon of cheese.

Enough for about 8 crostini

1 cup roasted cremini mushrooms (see page 42), finely chopped

2 tablespoons chopped flat-leaf parsley

⅛ teaspoon finely ground white pepper

¼ teaspoon fine sea salt

2 tablespoons grated Pecorino Romano, plus an additional teaspoon for each crostini

¼ cup olive oil

1 teaspoon white truffle oil

CHAPTER 3

SANDWICHES & SOUPS

We owe a debt to New York's Sullivan Street Bakery (and its offshoot, Grandaisy Bakery). When guests sit down at our restaurants, they are served thick slices of Sullivan's Pugliese loaf—a rustic, country bread with a crackly, crusty, deeply browned exterior and an interior of chewy crumb, scattershot with gaping holes and tiny bubbles. This is placed on the table with a saucer of our olive oil. When it comes to sandwiches, we rely on another Sullivan Street Bakery product: pizza bianca. This flatbread is crisp, flat but airy, and clearly Roman in its inspiration (if you've eaten pizza in the Campo de' Fiori in Rome, you know the stuff). It's more a relative of focaccia than it is of gooier, cheesier Neapolitan-style pizza.

Castronovo served sandwiches on Sullivan's flatbread at the restaurant he ran before the Spuntino; Falcinelli did the same thing for himself at home. But if you don't have easy access to Roman-style pizza bianca (i.e., you don't live in New York City or Rome), you could instead buy Jim Lahey's book, *My Bread*, and use it to replicate the exact same bread as we use at the Spuntino. (You can also make sandwiches out of his topped pizzas—for example, a meatball sandwich made with potato-topped pizza bianca is super delicious.) Alternatively, you could substitute another dense and chewy bread—Italian ciabatta always works well—and forget about it. Either way, many of the sandwich combinations in the pages that follow are great ways to repurpose leftover Spuntino ingredients, so don't discount them just because of the bread.

This chapter also includes the hearty soups that are mainstays of our menu. All are easy, inexpensive to make, and good served hot or cold. Any of these soups could be a meal unto itself with a slice of bread and a glass of wine. Similarly, they're an excellent way to round out a spread.

SANDWICHES

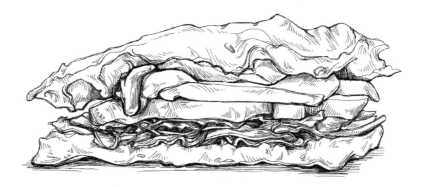

When the Spuntino was just getting on its feet, sandwiches were an important part of its success: They helped to lure in neighborhood folks during the day. Someone would come in for the first time, order a sandwich to-go, then the next time they'd roll over the stroller and eat it here, and soon enough afterward, they became regulars.

But for as loyal a fan base as our sandwiches have, there's one thing that needs to be said about them: they couldn't be easier.

MEAT & CHEESE COMBOS

For meat-and-cheese sandwiches, we go pretty basic: equal amounts of meat and cheese—and not too much of either. At Frankies, we typically use a little less than two ounces of meat and two ounces of cheese per sandwich, which means that if we start out with a half pound of each, we get four sandwiches out of the deal even if we're snacking as we make them. We like SOPRESSATA WITH PROVOLONE and PROSCIUTTO WITH PECORINO. We don't like to add mustard or mayonnaise to Italian meats and cheeses; we find that they just don't add to the experience. All you need to do is get really delicious meat and cheese. No prepackaged stuff from the supermarket: go to a place where the counter guy will slice it fresh.

If we were going to gussy up the meat-and-cheese basics, it would be with a drizzle of olive oil, with ripe tomato in the height of the summer, or with a pickled item from the antipasto selection at your local deli, like roasted red peppers or artichokes in oil, chopped up and added with a sparing hand.

SUPER-SIMPLE SANDWICHES

The **Bacon, Lettuce & Tomato** starts with **2 tablespoons of Hellmann's mayonnaise,** 1 tablespoon for the top slice and 1 for the bottom. Then **4 slices of ripe tomato** (cut ¼-inch thick, each slice seasoned with salt and black pepper) and **2 big leaves of romaine** go on the top slice. We put **4 slices of thick-cut bacon** (cooked on a rimmed baking sheet in 350°F oven for 15 minutes—it should still have a little chew to it) on the bottom and stick the two halves together.

The **Sicilian Tuna,** which is practically a TLT, is very similar. It starts with **2 tablespoons of Hellmann's mayonnaise,** 1 tablespoon for the top slice and 1 for the bottom. Then **4 slices of ripe tomato** (cut ¼-inch thick, each slice seasoned with salt and black pepper) and **1 loosely packed cup of arugula** go on the top slice. We put **⅓ cup of oil-packed Sicilian tuna** (with the oil drained off), flaked with a fork, on the bottom piece of bread; top it with **¼ cup thinly sliced red onion,** a little salt, and a couple twists of **white pepper.** Then stick the two halves together.

Our **Mozzarella, Tomato & Red Pepper** sandwich is just like it sounds: **four ¼-inch-thick slices of mozzarella,** topped with **four ¼-inch-thick slices of ripe tomato,** topped with **4 or 5 thin, long strips of roasted red pepper.** (If your deli has good ones, buy them there. Otherwise they're a cinch to make.) Top that combo with **1 loosely packed cup of arugula** and you're done.

LEFTOVERS BETWEEN BREAD

The **Roasted Vegetable** sandwich is this: **2 cups of Roasted Vegetable Salad** (page 72). That's it—and leftover salad is perfectly good for the sandwich. (At the restaurant we make it fresh, but at the restaurant that's easy.) This sandwich, and the salad that spawned it, are a compelling reason to make the vegetable antipasti on pages 34–45 in quantities as large as easily manageable: they can serve as antipasti or side dishes on night one, a salad on day two and, if there's anything left, a sandwich on day three. That's putting your kitchen time to good use.

If all you have is some leftover broccoli rabe, you're half the way to a SAUSAGE & BROCCOLI RABE SANDWICH. (Same goes if you've got leftover sausage.) **Three roughly chopped stalks Broccoli Rabe** (cooked as directed on page 38) is enough to dress a sausage sandwich. We par-cook the sausage as for the cavatelli on page 102, but instead of slicing them into coins, we slice them in half lengthwise (usually **two sausages** to a sandwich, but the sausages we buy are little quarter-pound guys) and brown the cut side in a pan with a little oil. Stick it on the sandwich bread, warm up the rabe in the sausage fat in the pan, and put it on top of the meat. Top the rabe with **1 tablespoon grated Pecorino** cheese and serve.

And then there's the MEATBALL MARINARA: **2 Meatballs** (see pages 124–27), lightly smushed with the back of a spoon into the bottom piece of bread. Topped with **¼ cup tomato sauce,** very warm to hot. Topped with **2 tablespoons grated Pecorino** cheese. No one is going to say that adding 4 thin slices of fresh and creamy mozzarella is a bad idea, but we only do that occasionally. Just think about this sandwich the next time you're thinking of making meatballs: It always pays off to make more than you need, because they keep in the sauce for days in the fridge and make a really delicious and filling sandwich.

One sandwich that straddles the leftover zone and the very, very rare realm of sandwiches we'll spend all day cooking to eat is our EGGPLANT MARINARA WITH MOZZARELLA. It is made with the Eggplant Marinara from page 137, though at the restaurant we typically offer only the eggplant as a sandwich— not as an entrée. Whether you cook the eggplant expressly for sandwiches or use leftovers to make them, the formula, from the bottom up is **1 cup Eggplant Marinara** (scoop it out of the baking pan, roughly chop it, and warm it up until too hot to the touch in a small skillet over low heat) topped with a blanket of **¼-inch-thick slices of mozzarella,** about 4 per sandwich.

SOUPS

ROASTED BUTTERNUT SQUASH SOUP

We take a less-is-more approach to squash soup. When we're eating it, we want the most vegetable and the least amount of anything else. The sweet potato isn't absolutely necessary, but it helps get the consistency right, especially if the squash is watery.

Serves 4 to 6

1. Heat the oven to 350°F. Coat the squash and sweet potato with a light slick of olive oil and season with salt and pepper.

2. Arrange the squash cut side up on a baking sheet, stick the half potato on there with it, and roast for 1 hour, or until both are very tender. Let cool slightly.

3. When the vegetables are cool enough to handle, scoop the flesh from the skins and combine in a blender. Add a large pinch of salt, the pepper, the five-spice powder, water, and honey and blend until smooth. Taste and add more honey if you want it sweeter or a tiny pinch more of five-spice powder to round out the flavor.

4. Pour the soup into a pot and reheat, then ladle it into bowls, nice and hot.

1 butternut squash (2 to 2½ pounds), halved and seeded

½ sweet potato

A couple of splashes of olive oil

Fine sea salt

Freshly ground white pepper

½ teaspoon Chinese five-spice powder, or more to taste

1 cup water

1 teaspoon honey, or more to taste

Wanna dress it up? Drizzle the soup with pumpkinseed oil just before serving.

ESCAROLE & CANNELLINI BEAN SOUP

Everybody's grandma made this fixture of the southern Italian immigrant kitchen. Add some short pasta to it and it's pasta fagiola—and then it's dinner for sure.

One thing we'd encourage you to try: eating the leftovers cold. We haven't eaten this soup hot in years. We roll into the restaurant in the morning, pull the soup out of the fridge, ladle ourselves out big bowls, and douse them with olive oil, sea salt, and chopped parsley (and sometimes cheese and tomato sauce as well). It's delicious and great fuel for a long day.

Serves 6

2 cups (12 ounces) dried cannellini beans

¼ cup olive oil, plus additional for garnish

1 medium onion, finely chopped

1 stalk celery, finely chopped

1 small carrot, finely chopped

Fine sea salt

Freshly ground white pepper

Red pepper flakes

8 cups Vegetable Broth (page 14)

1 bay leaf

1. Put the beans in a bowl, cover with water, and soak for at least 8 hours or as long as overnight, replacing the water once or twice during the soak. Drain and pick over the beans for stones or pebbles before cooking them.

2. Heat 2 tablespoons of the olive oil in a wide, deep soup pot (an enameled Dutch oven is perfect) over medium heat. After a minute, add the onion, celery, and carrot, and season them with pinches of salt, a few turns of white pepper, and red pepper flakes to taste. Sauté the aromatics, stirring regularly, until the onion is going golden, the celery is translucent, and the carrot is softened, 12 to 15 minutes.

3. Add the beans, broth, and bay leaf to the pot and bring to a boil, then reduce the heat so the beans simmer gently. Cook for 2 hours or until they're soft but not disintegrating. (At this point, you could cool the beans in their cooking liquid and refrigerate them for a day or two or freeze them for up to a month.)

4. Meanwhile, heat the remaining 2 tablespoons olive oil in an 8-inch sauté pan over low heat. After a minute, add the garlic and cook it slowly for 8 to 10 minutes, until it has gone a pale gold and is sweetly aromatic, maybe starting to brown the tiniest bit around the edges.

5. When the garlic is good to go, turn the heat to medium-high and add a pinch of red pepper flakes. Cook for 30 seconds, then add the escarole, piling it as high as it needs to go. Add a large pinch of salt and a few turns of white pepper and toss to coat the escarole in some of the oil in the pan. Cover the pan and cook for 4 minutes.

6. Remove the lid and toss the escarole again. It should be wilted and greener than it was when it started, and the water and oil should have melded together into a nice, juicy pan sauce. Add the escarole to the beans.

7. Serve the soup hot or chill it and ladle it out cold. Finish each bowl with a splash of olive oil, a few turns of white pepper, and a couple of tablespoons of grated cheese, regardless of the temperature. (That said, if you're eating it cold, chopped parsley, added in abundance, is very good for it.)

2 cloves garlic, cut lengthwise in half

1 or 2 heads escarole, cut into 1-inch pieces (3 to 4 cups)

½ cup grated Pecorino Romano

LENTIL SOUP
WITH SMOKED BACON

Lentil soup is one of those Depression-era classics (for more about lentils, see page 15). If you have lentils and water and a scrap of meat, you've got a meal, and everything else is gravy. We like bacon as the meat to flavor this soup, but you could use almost anything—prosciutto ends, ham hocks, whatever you have lying around.

If you have the time, making it with vegetable broth will add an extra nuance, another layer of flavor, to the soup. And if you lose the bacon and turn the soup vegan, you definitely want to make it with vegetable broth.

Serves 6

2 cups (12 ounces) lentils

1 slice bacon, thinly sliced

1 medium onion, finely chopped

1 stalk celery, finely chopped

1 small carrot, finely chopped

1 plump clove garlic, thinly sliced

8 cups Vegetable Broth (page 14) or water

1 bay leaf

Fine sea salt and freshly ground black pepper

1. Put the lentils in a bowl, cover with water, and soak for at least 8 hours, or as long as overnight, replacing the water once or twice during the soak.

2. Drain the lentils well and pick them over for any stones or other debris that might have made it into the mix.

3. Heat a wide, deep soup pot (an enameled Dutch oven is perfect) over medium heat. After a minute, add the bacon. Cook, stirring, until the bacon fat is beginning to render, about 3 minutes. Add the onion, celery, carrot, and garlic and sauté the aromatics until the onion is going golden, the celery is translucent, and the carrot is softened, 12 to 15 minutes.

4. Add the lentils, vegetable broth, and bay leaf to the pot. Bring the pot to a boil, then reduce the heat to low and simmer for 45 minutes, until the lentils are tender but not mushy.

5. Discard the bay leaf. Before ladling the soup into serving bowls, season it to taste with salt. (Depending on the saltiness of your bacon, the soup may not need it.) The soup can be prepared a day ahead and stored, covered, in the refrigerator. Offer fresh black pepper at the table.

CHAPTER 4

SALADS

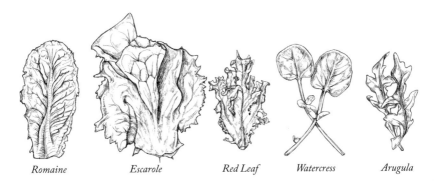

Romaine *Escarole* *Red Leaf* *Watercress* *Arugula*

We love long-simmered meatballs and hearty pastas, but if there's one thing we like to think we do right at the Spuntino, it's salad.

Good salads start with good ingredients. Limp lettuce should be cooked if it is to be eaten at all. Flat-tasting oil will kill even the best-planned salad. Old cheese has no place in a salad or at the table, except in Cheese Broth (see page 14). A similar sort of pronouncement could be made about everything that's going to end up in the salad bowl: nuts, raw or cooked vegetables, and even the black pepper you'll pass at the table.

Salads need not be complicated, fussy affairs. One of our favorite Spuntino salads is one of the simplest: half a lobe of runny mozzarella di bufala, as fresh and creamy as possible, with a couple of handfuls of peppery, tender arugula. We dress the greens with a splash of our own olive oil, a dash of red wine vinegar, and a pinch of salt; and we grind black pepper over the salad at the table. That's it.

If you can buy good mozzarella and arugula and have a modestly outfitted pantry, the salad is practically made by the time you're checking out at the store. Add a little time in the kitchen between the store and the table, and you can do even more.

MAKING A GOOD SALAD

There are a few kitchen practices that we think are important to making the best salad possible.

STORE THE GREENS RIGHT

Salad greens should be refrigerated in a lightly humidified spot. Refrigerators often have a special drawer for them that does the trick (the crisper); otherwise, we find that they keep best in paper bags like those our neighborhood grocer uses; the water clinging to the greens dampens the bag slightly and creates the right environment. Always keep heads of lettuce intact until just before washing and using them.

SPIN, SPIN, SPIN

Get yourself a salad spinner if you don't have one. It'll be twenty of the best dollars you've ever spent. Salad spinners are essential for washing and drying lettuces properly, and clean, dry lettuce can be the difference between an edible salad and a memorable salad.

To do it right: Put the lettuce (prepared as directed in the recipe) in the salad spinner and fill the spinner with cold water. Occasionally swirl the greens in the water as the bowl fills. Let the greens float in the water for a few moments, then lift the strainer out of the bowl; any dirt will fall to the bottom of the bowl. Discard the water and repeat until there's no grit left behind.

Next: spin, spin, spin (dumping water from the bowl between cycles) until you can open the spinner and pull out a perfectly dry leaf.

DRESS SALADS IN THE WIDEST BOWL POSSIBLE

The goal is an evenly and lightly dressed salad, right? If you cram a bunch of greens into a small bowl, drizzle them with a vinaigrette, and then repeatedly jam your tongs into the bowl to "toss" the salad, you're going to bruise the greens, and more likely than not end up with an unevenly dressed salad— some leaves drenched, some dry, none just right.

So get a big, wide bowl, at least a foot in diameter. Wider, shallower bowls are preferable to deeper, taller ones. We like the ones with a large, nearly flat bottom that you can buy inexpensively at restaurant supply stores. Add your dressing to the bowl (it's smart to hold back a little, because you can always add more), then add the greens. Toss lightly but thoroughly. No tongs in the salad bowl, either: the best tools, and the only ones you can ensure aren't going to crush the greens, are located at the end of your arms.

Never, ever dress in advance; salads should be dressed as close to serving time as possible.

BASIC VINAIGRETTES

Our basic vinaigrettes are simple and versatile. One is a wine vinaigrette with a dash of mustard (see page 68). Classic. We use it to dress arugula, which is spicy enough to match the pungent accent the vinegar and mustard lend to the vinaigrette. The other is the Cipollini Onion Vinaigrette (page 70), our adapation of a white onion vinaigrette Castronovo picked up when he was cooking at Hotel Schloss Reinach in Freiburg, Germany (where he met and married his wife, Heike). It was the basic dressing for the green salad there as well as the sauce the kitchen would use to amp up any of the *bilage*—simple vegetable side dishes like raw cabbage or roasted carrots—that might accompany a meal.

Both of these basic vinaigrettes rely on the lecithin found in commonplace ingredients—mustard and onions—to keep them emulsified. Both are best mixed in a blender, which gives the finished dressing a glossy, smooth texture.

A salad dressing should be delicious on its own—good enough to drink. Taste and retaste a dressing until you're happy with it.

RED WINE VINAIGRETTE

*Makes a little less
than 1 cup, enough
for 6 to 8 salads*

**2 tablespoons
Dijon mustard**

**2 tablespoons red
wine vinegar**

**¼ cup hot tap
water**

**¼ cup
grapeseed oil**

**5 turns
white pepper**

**Large pinch of
fine sea salt**

**Tiniest drip
of honey**

**2 tablespoons
olive oil**

Combine all the ingredients in a blender and purée until emulsified. The color of the dressing should be uniform and the texture silky smooth. Check the seasoning and adjust as necessary. Use immediately or keep, covered, in the fridge for as short a time as possible (and no longer than 24 hours).

ARUGULA, PECORINO & RED WINE VINAIGRETTE SALAD

Falcinelli likes to tell the story about how Michelangelo said that he saw David in the stone before he began to work on his famous sculpture. All he had to do, the artist said, was to chisel away the excess stone.

This utterly simple and absolutely delicious arugula/cheese/vinaigrette combination is just as obvious, at least to us. It doesn't need anything fancy. But just like it took the right stone to make David, this salad will elude you if all the ingredients aren't right: peppery and pert arugula, fresh Pecorino cheese (not that chunk that's been hiding in the back of your fridge for months), and just-made vinaigrette are the components that add up to success.

Combine all the ingredients. Then toss, taste and check for seasoning, and plate. Offer freshly ground black pepper at the table.

For each salad:

2 ounces (1 loosely packed quart) arugula, any long or tough stems trimmed

2 tablespoons Red Wine Vinaigrette (opposite)

3 thinly sliced triangles Pecorino Romano

CIPOLLINI ONION VINAIGRETTE

We use cipollini onions because they're sweet, and they give the dressing a vaguely Italian bent, but yellow and white onions work just fine if you can't get your hands on the little guys.

Makes a little less than 1 cup, enough for about 6 salads

⅓ cup roughly chopped meaty cipollini onion or other variety

1 teaspoon Dijon mustard

2 tablespoons red wine vinegar

Drop of honey

5 turns white pepper

Juice of ½ lemon (a tablespoon or so)

½ cup grapeseed oil

Large pinch fine sea salt

2 tablespoons olive oil

Combine all the ingredients in a blender, adding the olive oil last—after everything is pretty much all ground up and headed toward liquidville—and process until smooth. Use immediately or keep, covered, in the fridge for as short a time as possible (and no longer than 24 hours).

FRANKIES GREENS

Frankies Greens is what we call our basic salad: mesclun, dressing, maybe a roasted mushroom or carrot from the antipasto station to add some color. It's as easy to make as the dressing, because that's all you need to put a salad on the table.

Toss the greens with the vinaigrette, taste and check for seasoning, and plate. Offer freshly ground black pepper at the table.

Serves 4

2 ounces (1 loosely packed quart) mixed greens

2 tablespoons Cipollini Onion Vinaigrette (opposite)

If there's any work to be done, it's in making sure your mesclun isn't mushy soft. Taste it at the grocery store, right there in the vegetable aisle, or farmers' market. It should have crunch and sweetness, like all fresh lettuce. Though be warned: a lot of mesclun mixes tend toward limpness. If sad mixed lettuces are the only ones available to you, look to other recipes in this section for salad guidance.

Roasted Vegetable Salad

This recipe has its roots in the earliest days of the Spuntino when we were first working with all these sheet trays of delicious, healthy roasted vegetables around. On mornings after a night of heavy eating or drinking, we'd wolf down a bowl of roasted beets for breakfast. In the middle of a hectic day, we'd sneak downstairs to the basement prep kitchen and toss a bunch of roasted vegetables with vinaigrette, to be scarfed down while standing, before running back upstairs to cook.

After a couple of weeks of eating like that, we realized we should probably share our kitchen snack with our customers. We fine-tuned it, and that's how this salad and the Roasted Vegetable Sandwich (page 57)—this salad stuck between slices of sandwich bread—got on the menu. They've proved popular enough that we can't take them off, and they're a great way to make roasted vegetables go further.

Which is how we would approach this salad at home. First, we'd make a selection of roasted vegetables for an antipasto spread to accompany a dinner. Then, sometime in the following couple of days, we'd throw the leftover vegetables together into this salad. In that case, you would want extra cups of leftover vegetables (which is quite a bit). This recipe is the exact mix of roast vegetables we serve at the restaurant.

Factor in an hour or so of work to clean, prepare, cook and season this quantity of vegetables.

1. Chop the roasted vegetables and combine in a large mixing bowl and toss them to mix well. Factor in an hour or so of work to clean, prepare, cook, and season this quantity of vegetables.

2. Combine the vinegar, oil, vinaigrette (if using), salt, and white pepper in a small mixing bowl and whisk well to blend.

3. Drizzle the dressing over the vegetables, then mix them with clean hands, gently but thoroughly, until they are coated. Portion the salad among four salad bowls and serve, offering black pepper from the grinder at the table.

Serves 4

Any combination of roasted vegetables (see pages 34–45) would work. Try this combo:

1 pound green beans (or 2 bunches broccoli rabe)

1 bunch small carrots

1 medium head cauliflower

2 or 3 meaty beets or 1 bunch small beets

One 8- to 10-ounce package cremini mushrooms

DRESSING

¼ cup balsamic vinegar

¼ cup olive oil

2 tablespoons Cipollini Onion Vinaigrette (page 70; optional but nice)

Large pinch of fine sea salt

10 turns white pepper

Black pepper

SHAVED RAW BRUSSELS SPROUTS WITH CASTELROSSO

Brussels sprouts aren't the first ingredient anybody thinks of when they think of Italian food, but this salad takes a basic equation from the Italian kitchen—fresh vegetables, olive oil, and a little bit of Italian cheese—and makes the sprouts work in the context of the cuisine. It's also a healthier, fresher salad for the winter months.

Serves 4

2 pints Brussels sprouts

½ cup plus 1 tablespoon olive oil

½ cup freshly squeezed lemon juice

½ teaspoon fine sea salt

¼ teaspoon freshly ground white pepper

1 cup crumbled Castelrosso cheese (about 4 ounces)

Black pepper

1. Discard any dark or limp leaves from the Brussels sprouts and trim off their bottoms. Cut the sprouts in half through the core and then slice them crosswise, taking time to slice them as thin as possible. We call them "shaved" raw Brussels sprouts, which says how thin we like them, so make sure you use a sharp knife.

2. Transfer the Brussels sprouts to a mixing bowl. (You can shave the Brussels sprouts up to a couple of hours in advance and keep them covered in the refrigerator until you're ready to serve them.)

3. Whisk together the olive oil, lemon juice, salt, and white pepper in a large, wide mixing bowl. Add the shredded Brussels sprouts to the bowl by the handful, tossing all the while. Once you've dressed the sprouts, portion them out into salad bowls, top each salad with ¼ cup of the crumbled cheese, and serve. Offer black pepper from the grinder at the table.

WATERCRESS WITH FRESH FIGS & GORGONZOLA

This one is super-simple: peppery watercress; pungent, salty Gorgonzola; and the sweetness of fruit to bring them together. We prefer hydroponically grown watercress—which has thinner stems and larger, more delicate leaves—if you can find it.

Put the greens in a wide, deep salad bowl. Sprinkle them with the salt, toss; season them with the white pepper, toss; drizzle them with the vinaigrette, toss. Divide the greens among serving plates and top each salad with a quarter of the cheese and 4 fig quarters. Serve.

VARIATIONS: Whenever peaches are in season, we use them in place of the figs in this salad. They're a perfect foil for the cheese. Figure on about half a peach per salad, cut into wedges. Cut the peaches in your hand with a paring knife, Grandma-style, right over the mixing bowl so you don't lose any of their juices.

After peaches, we go to ripe figs and then, in the late fall and early winter when the ripe fig supply has withered, we turn to dried figs. You can, too. Soak them overnight first. If they're large figs that plump up to the size of ripe fresh fruit, use them the same way: 1 per salad, quartered. Double the quantity if they're smaller. Easy.

In deep winter we puree dried figs (pick off any stems) with balsamic vinegar and honey to taste, then smear the puree in the bottom of the salad bowl and put the salad on top of it. Very nice. Offer black pepper from the grinder at the table.

Serves 4

8 ounces watercress (4 loosely packed cups per serving), bottom half inch of stems trimmed

⅛ teaspoon fine sea salt

6 to 8 turns white pepper

6 tablespoons Cipollini Onion Vinaigrette (page 70)

4 ounces Gorgonzola, cut into wedges (or whatever shape your chunk of Gorgonzola lends itself to being apportioned)

4 ripe black Mission figs, cut into quarters

ROMAINE HEARTS WITH CAESAR SALAD DRESSING

Back in the early 1990s, Falcinelli ran his own restaurant, Culinary Renaissance, in Metuchen, New Jersey. This salad dressing was one of the recipes he developed in the kitchen there (it was part of a consulting gig for a fast-food chain on the West Coast), and it's been a fixture on his menus ever since.

Note that it's a recipe for Caesar salad dressing, not a traditional Caesar salad. Traditional Caesars, made with raw eggs and croutons, *can* be awesome. But a traditional Caesar is a labor of love that needs to be undertaken by a person who knows what they're doing. This is a foolproof way to put a delicious salad on the table—and to take the raw eggs out of the equation for safety's sake.

Also note that the recipe calls for Hellmann's mayonnaise. Sometimes there's no substitute. The deli where Falcinelli worked as a teenager went through hundreds of gallons every week, and when he was in his thirties, working with chef Nobu Matsuhisa, he learned that Nobu also used Hellmann's for his signature dishes like fried rock shrimp and lobster with mayo. Hellmann's might not have the *oooh-la-la* fancy appeal of handmade mayo, but it's great stuff.

1. Trim the root ends from the romaine, separate the leaves, and wash and dry them. Put the lettuce in the fridge to chill while you prepare the dressing.

2. Combine ¼ cup of the Pecorino with the remaining ingredients (except the black pepper) in a blender and puree until the dressing is smooth. (If you don't have a blender, mince the garlic and anchovy, and whisk them together with the rest of the dressing ingredients.) Taste and add salt if necessary; the cheese, Hellmann's, Worcestershire, and anchovies are all salty, so you probably won't need any additional salt. Loosen the dressing with water as needed starting with the prescribed ¼ cup.

3. Toss the chilled lettuce with the dressing in a large bowl. Transfer to serving plates or a serving platter and finish with a generous crowning of the remaining grated cheese and a few turns of black pepper. Serve at once.

Serves 4 to 6

3 hearts of romaine (pull away the floppiest, greenest outer leaves)

⅓ cup grated Pecorino Romano, plus additional cheese for serving

½ cup Hellmann's mayonnaise

¼ cup water

1½ teaspoons red wine vinegar

1 garlic clove

2 anchovy fillets

¼ teaspoon Worcestershire sauce

¼ teaspoon Tabasco

8 turns freshly ground white pepper

Fine sea salt, if needed

Freshly ground black pepper

ESCAROLE WITH SLICED RED ONION & WALNUTS

This is one of our heartiest salads. With a spread of cured meats and some good bread, it makes a good midday meal (one at which Castronovo will inevitably start making escarole salad roll-ups, wrapping up pinches of the salad in slices of prosciutto or speck).

It's our go-to salad in the winter. Escarole and the heartier greens of the chicory family do better in wintertime greenhouses, and the California walnuts we use are freshest in the fall and winter (the California harvest ends in November).

When we're feeling flush, we use Fiore Sardo cheese to finish the salad. It's softer and sweeter than our standard grating cheese, Pecorino Romano, but if you can't find Fiore Sardo, regular Pecorino will do just fine. If you're looking for additional heft, a poached egg with a runny yolk is an excellent addition.

Serves 4

2 small or 1 large head escarole

1 cup very, very thinly sliced red onion

1 cup walnuts, crumbled by hand

¾ cup Walnut Dressing (recipe follows)

1. Discard the bitter dark green outer leaves of the escarole. Core the head and float it in a salad spinner full of water for a minute, then drain and spin it dry. Coarsely chop the escarole into manageable pieces. Prepare the Walnut Dressing. (It can be made a day in advance.)

2. Toss the escarole with the red onion and walnuts in a large salad bowl. Dress it with the Walnut Dressing and the walnut oil, tossing well to make sure the salad is evenly and lightly dressed.

3. Serve the salad in the bowl, or divide it among serving plates. Finish with curls of Fiore Sardo and offer fresh black pepper at the table.

1 tablespoon walnut oil

½ cup loosely packed Fiore Sardo or Pecorino Romano cut into curls with a vegetable peeler

Black pepper

WALNUT DRESSING

Combine all the ingredients in a blender and puree until emulsified. The color of the dressing should be uniform and the texture silky smooth. Check the seasoning and adjust as necessary. Use immediately or keep, covered, in the fridge for as short a time as possible (and no longer than 24 hours).

Makes a little less than 1 cup, enough for 6 to 8 salads

¼ cup walnut halves, crushed

1 teaspoon honey

1 tablespoon walnut oil

¼ cup grapeseed oil

1 tablespoon tap water

2 tablespoons red wine vinegar

Salt and freshly ground white pepper, to taste

Puntarelle with Lemon, Capers, Anchovy & Pecorino Romano

This is an Italian salad you see everywhere—on outdoor tables at trattorias in Rome, or under the Manhattan sun on the wide swath of sidewalk outside Bar Pitti. It's the Italian way of bending the bitterness of greens like puntarelle into submission. In the early spring, you can substitute dandelion greens for puntarelle.

Serves 4

1 large or 2 smaller heads puntarelle

2 anchovy fillets

2 teaspoons capers, soaked

½ clove garlic

½ cup olive oil

Juice of 1 lemon, or more to taste

Freshly ground white pepper

½ bunch flat-leaf parsley leaves, chopped

¼ cup grated Pecorino Romano, plus more

Black pepper

1. Separate and wash the greens in cold water, then spin dry. Cut off the extremities: the harshly bitter green tips and the woody white bottom ends. Coarsely chop the remaining greens into manageable lengths.

2. Chop the anchovies, capers, and garlic into a near paste. (Roughly chop each one, then combine and work over the pile with your knife.) Transfer the paste to a bowl, add the olive oil, lemon juice, and white pepper to taste, and whisk together. Taste and add more lemon juice if needed, then stir in the parsley and cheese.

3. Toss the puntarelle with the dressing and divide the salad among serving plates. Scatter with the grated cheese. Offer black pepper and additional cheese at the table.

Tomato, Avocado & Red Onion Salad

Falcinelli loves to say that this salad "makes gazpacho in your mouth." It's funny, because there are no avocados in gazpacho, but true because the experience of eating it—it's all lush and creamy with super-fresh tomato flavor—is gazpacho-like. The sting and the acid from the raw onion keep it from going flabby.

Serves 4

2 large ripe tomatoes

1 small (or ½ medium) red onion, thinly sliced

Fine sea salt

¼ cup extra virgin olive oil, plus more for drizzling

2 tablespoons red wine vinegar

2 Hass avocados

Freshly ground black pepper

1. Core the tomatoes and slice into wedges. Combine with the sliced onion, a large pinch of salt, and the olive oil and vinegar in a large bowl. Gently toss, and divide among four serving plates.

2. Halve, pit, peel, and slice the avocados and divide among the four plates. Sprinkle the avocado with a small pinch of salt and drizzle each plate with a little olive oil. Finish with a few grinds of black pepper just before the salad goes to the table.

BUYING TOMATOES

In the early summer, we make this salad with ripe red Roma plum tomatoes. But as soon as heirloom tomatoes make their way to the local markets, we switch to them and ride that train for as long as possible. There's no need to worry much about the exact heirloom variety—just buy the best you can find and give them time to ripen if they need it.

ROASTED BEET & AVOCADO SALAD

We've never seen an avocado on a trip to Italy. (Maybe in Sicily? Some trips leave hazier memories than others.) And we didn't eat them growing up in Queens, not at home or when we visited our grandmas' houses.

But we both love avocados. When we're on health food kicks or raw food cleanses, we eat them straight from the skin, dressed with olive oil and salt. When we're not, we're always happy to kill a few orders of guacamole with tortilla chips. And there's nothing as natural, as healthy and affordable, that adds the same luxurious richness to a meal.

Avocados work perfectly with beets. Beets are earthy and crazy sweet, and the fruity fattiness of the avocado grounds them. This is a perfect simple salad for the wintertime when storage beets are around, good avocados are coming in from California, and real tomatoes are either months behind or ahead of us.

SHOPPING FOR AVOCADOS

Some people can go to the market and feel their way around the avocado bin until they find the one perfectly ripe, ready-to-eat specimen. Most can't. And unless you're in a real hurry (in which case you're looking for an avocado with no obvious discoloration that gives easily to a gentle squeeze) it's always better to buy unripe avocados and let them ripen at home on the counter.

When buying avocados to ripen at home, look for fruit that is uniformly firm and heavy for its size. Bring it home and wait. (Another advantage of buying unripe avocados is that they won't get turned into guacamole in your grocery bags the way ripe ones sometimes do.)

In one to three days, the avocado will ripen to that point of gentle, yielding tenderness, and when it does, use it immediately. Ripe avocados don't like to hang around long before getting overripe. Meanwhile, why not try to grow your own avocado tree? We're serious (see page 210).

1. Prepare the avocados. Run a knife lengthwise all the way around each avocado, then twist it to separate the two halves. Lightly hack into the pit stuck in one of the halves with the blade of the knife, then twist it and pull out the pit. Slide a spoon down the side of each avocado half, between the flesh and the skin, and trace the contour and shape of the fruit to free the flesh from the skin. Cut the flesh into 1-inch chunks. Handle the avocados gently: nobody likes bruised and discolored avocados, and you're not making guacamole here.

2. Combine the avocado and beets in a large mixing bowl. Whisk together the vinegar, olive oil, vinaigrette, salt, and white pepper in a small bowl. Pour the dressing over the beets and avocados, tossing gently until the salad is evenly dressed. Divide among four salad bowls, hit each portion with a generous speckling of black pepper, and serve at once.

Serves 4

2 ripe avocados

4 cups chopped roasted beets (see page 37)

6 tablespoons balsamic vinegar

¼ cup olive oil

3 tablespoons Cipollini Onion Vinaigrette (page 70), or substitute an additional 2 tablespoons olive oil and another tablespoon of red wine vinegar, and increase the salt to 1 teaspoon)

¾ teaspoon fine sea salt

20 turns white pepper

Freshly ground black pepper

Fennel, Celery Root, Parsley & Red Onion Salad with Lemon & Olive Oil

Although we make it all year round, this salad is really a godsend in the winter when you're looking for that refreshing fresh-vegetable crunch and something bright and light. The two things that make it stand out: the amount of parsley—it should practically be a parsley salad, with the other vegetables lending it texture—and the finishing touch of pumpkinseed oil, which, combined with the white pepper in the dressing, gives a depth of flavor to the salad.

Serves 4

½ celery root

1 fennel bulb, with stems removed

⅔ cup sliced red onion

2 packed cups flat-leaf parsley leaves

¼ cup olive oil, or more to taste

Juice of ½ lemon

½ teaspoon fine sea salt

16 turns white pepper

Pumpkinseed oil, for drizzling (optional)

Pecorino Romano, to taste

1. Peel the celery root and cut it into fine julienne. Trim the fennel bulb, discarding tough stems and reserving any fresh, pert fronds to garnish the salad, and julienne. (You should have in the neighborhood of 2 cups of each.)

2. Toss the cut vegetables together with the parsley in a large bowl. Add the oil, lemon juice, salt, and white pepper and toss again. Taste and add more oil, salt, and/or lemon juice as needed.

3. Divide the salad among serving plates. Finish each with a drizzle of pumpkinseed oil and a few curls of Pecorino Romano (cut with a vegetable peeler) and serve.

RADISH SALAD WITH PARSLEY, CAPERS & ANCHOVIES

Radishes come in many shapes and sizes and different generosities of bundling, but in most cases one large bunch of radishes will feed 4 people.

Serves 4

1 to 2 bunches radishes

2 anchovy fillets, minced

1½ teaspoons minced capers

1 plump clove garlic, minced

6 tablespoons finely chopped flat-leaf parsley

6 tablespoons olive oil, plus more for drizzling

Grated zest of ¼ lemon (use a Microplane)

A couple of large pinches coarse sea salt

Freshly ground white pepper (8 to 10 turns)

12 to 16 very thin slices ricotta salata (no more than ¼ pound)

1. Trim off the radish greens and scrub the radishes well. Cut them in half through the root, then lay them cut side down on the cutting board and cut them into wedges, 4 to 6 wedges per half radish. Put the radishes in a large salad bowl.

2. Combine the anchovies, capers, garlic, and parsley in a small mixing bowl. Add the olive oil and stir to combine, then add the lemon zest and stir again.

3. Add the dressing to the radishes and toss well. Hit them with coarse salt and white pepper and toss again. Portion the salad among serving bowls or heap it up high on a platter. Drizzle with olive oil (the more, as always, the merrier), and neatly arrange the thinly sliced ricotta salata over the top.

SARDINE, BLOOD ORANGE & PUNTARELLE SALAD

Wintertime party-time good-time salad from Frank Castronovo: a salad to impress.

Serves 6

1 lemon, halved

⅓ cup olive oil

Large pinch of fine sea salt

10 turns white pepper

2 bunches puntarelle, washed, trimmed (as described on page 80), and torn into nice bite-sized pieces

12 Cured Sardines (recipe follows)

2 blood oranges or the seeds of 1 pomegranate (see box opposite)

1. Squeeze the juice of the lemon into a small bowl or a measuring cup with a spout, or whatever you feel like using to mix your salad dressing in. Do it in a pint glass if you want to. Add the olive oil, salt, white pepper, and, if you're feeling adventurous, a couple of tablespoons of oil from the marinated sardines. Whisk the dressing until it looks nice. Set it aside.

2. Mound the puntarelle on a serving platter or on individual plates. Pull the sardines from their marinade one by one, letting the oil dribble off them, and arrange them over the greens in an attractive manner.

3. Fruit time: Slice off the top and bottom of each blood orange. Don't cut off too much, just enough so that you get the feel for how thick the peel and pith is and you have got a flat surface to set the citrus on when you cut it. Cut the skin away from the dark, sweet flesh with your knife, taking as much of the pith and as little of the fruit with it as possible. Cut out the individual segments of blood orange from the membranes that hold them together.

4. Scatter the fruit over the salad. Pour the dressing over all and serve.

CURED SARDINES

1. Pour the salt onto a plate. Put the vinegar in a shallow bowl large enough to accommodate the fillets. Have another container—what you'll cure/store them in—on hand. Dredge both sides of the fillets in the salt and let them sit for 10 minutes.

2. Brush most of the salt off the fillets and transfer them to the vinegar. Let them luxuriate in that for 15 minutes.

3. During some of that sitting-around time, combine 1 cup olive oil, the garlic, lemon zest and juice, parsley, and white pepper in the sardines' ultimate curing place.

4. Put the sardines in the marinade, add additional olive oil if needed to submerge them, and cover the dish with plastic wrap. Pop it into the refrigerator for 36 to 48 hours. (A little longer is fine; shorter is not.)

5. The sardines are ready to use as directed. Or just pull them out of the marinade, throw them skin side down on a hot grill, and char the skin a little bit, maybe 3 minutes tops. Squirt with lemon, sprinkle with salt, and eat hot. Serve only to good friends.

Makes enough for 6 salads or to serve 2 as a snack (see Step 5)

½ cup coarse sea salt or ⅓ cup fine sea salt

1 cup white wine vinegar or apple cider vinegar

6 fresh sardines, scaled and filleted

1 to 2 cups olive oil (enough to submerge the sardines)

2 cloves garlic, very finely minced

Grated zest and juice of 1 lemon

1 cup finely chopped flat-leaf parsley

10 turns white pepper

TO SUBSTITUTE POMEGRANATES IN SALAD

Cut the pomegranate in half in a bowl of cold water. After a minute or two, use your hands to break up the submerged pomegranate halves, liberating the ruby-red seeds from the dry white flesh. The seeds should sink; the flesh should float. Discard the flesh and drain the seeds. Scatter the fruit over the salad in place of the oranges, pour the dressing, and serve.

CHAPTER 5

PASTA

We make fresh pasta every day at the Spuntino: huge batches of gnocchi, cavatelli, and whatever noodles we've got on the menu at the time. The fridges are full of fresh pasta by the middle of the afternoon and then empty by midnight. When morning rolls around, it's time to make the pasta again.

Excepting some specials, all of our pasta dishes call for fresh pasta. This is not some purist or preference thing, but a matter of practicality: Our kitchen is so small that it's impossible for us to cook dried pasta fast enough to feed the crowds. (Dried pasta takes 7 or 8 or 9 minutes per batch, fresh pasta cooks in 2 or 3 minutes, and we have only three burners in the kitchen. The math's pretty easy.) Once the necessity of fresh pasta was established, we took to it with the eagerness of new converts.

That said, making pasta at home is a labor of love, something to do because you've got the time or inclination or are cooking a special dinner for friends or family. So we don't want you to feel like you're copping out if you swap high-quality Italian-made dried pasta for the freshly made stuff in these recipes. (We do the same thing at home, too.) Just increase the cooking time allotted for the noodles, and try to stick to the prescribed shapes in each recipe.

One more thing: making fresh pasta is not hard. It gets easier every time you do it. Force yourself to do it every day for a week, and it'll seem like second nature to you forever after.

FRESH PASTA

Fresh pasta needs to be fresh. That "fresh" stuff at the supermarket? That's not fresh. The "fresh" stuff they sell frozen at every Italian shop, even the ones that you love and that are great places, is not fresh enough either. Fresh pasta that you've made and then frozen? Not quite fresh enough (though frozen homemade cavatelli and gnocchi are pretty damn good).

If you're going to make fresh pasta, do it because you love it and you want to eat it and you want to serve it and you want to get into the primitive flour-into-food-on-the-table type of continuum.

ON THE PROCESS ITSELF—If you want noodles, you need a pasta machine. Yes, it is entirely possible to do it without one, but, really, it's the twenty-first century. Buy a hand-cranked Atlas pasta machine, and it will last you the rest of your natural life. If you can't afford one, stay in for the next few weeks and just make food out of this book and buy cheaper wine and take your lunch to work, and then you'll be able to. They're not expensive, and they make a world of difference.

If you've got a stand mixer, the pasta-making process is practically painless and almost entirely automatic. But stand mixers are a more serious investment, and the trusty old well method, described on pages 96–97, is fail-safe if labor-intensive. If you go for the hands-on, machine-free method, don't skimp on the kneading.

We're huge fans of cavatelli makers, too, cavatelli being about the simplest and most foolproof pasta to make at home. If you have the means, we recommend owning all the gear.

PASTAS TO MAKE AT HOME

Gnocchi

Cavatelli

Linguine

Fettuccine

Tagliatelle

Ravioli

PASTAS TO BUY

Spaghetti

Orecchiette

Lasagna

COOKING PASTA

The first step in any pasta recipe is to put water in a big pot and salt it. Nobody ever says how much salt to put in the water, because it's simple: the water should be salty, Atlantic Ocean salty. How do you know when there's enough salt in there? Taste it. Why "taste it" instead of giving a

PASTA SHAPES & SIZES

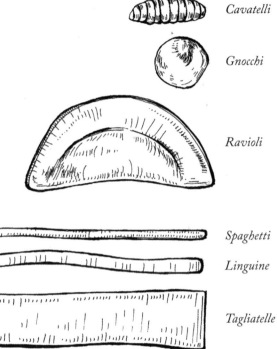

Cavatelli

Gnocchi

Ravioli

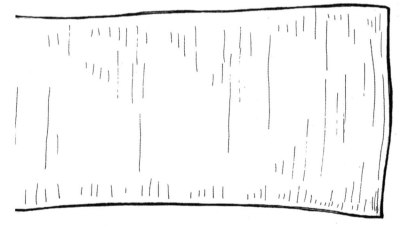

Spaghetti

Linguine

Tagliatelle

Lasagna

ratio? Because it's important to be in the habit of tasting whatever you're cooking—it's the only way you can make the minute adjustments that make all the difference. And why is salt important here? Because salt is water-soluble, and as the water enters the pasta, so does the salt, which makes the pasta taste like something.

When bringing a pot of water to a boil, cover it. A covered pot will boil faster because you're keeping the heat inside the pot instead of letting it waft off into the kitchen. And, no, there is no need to add oil to the pasta pot. It doesn't keep the pasta from sticking together; stirring once or twice about 30 seconds after adding it to the pot will do that.

The actual cooking is easy: boil the pasta as directed and drain well. Have a container of some kind in the sink to pour a little of the pasta cooking water into, should you need it to add to a sauce. After cooking it, give the pasta a 10-second rest before saucing it to let it blow off some steam and expel some water, so it soaks up more of the sauce.

A note about pasta cooking water: it's great to have on hand to loosen a sauce, but the water from cooking fresh pasta is nowhere near as good as the stuff from dried pasta. There's just something about that higher-gluten flour and all the extruding and drying the pasta's gone through that makes the cooking water better at emulsifying a sauce.

SAUCING PASTA

Another simple step. Decide on your approach: are you tossing the pasta with the sauce or pouring the sauce on top?

We do the restaurant style of saucing pasta at the Spuntino: combining the pasta and a more-or-less perfect amount of sauce in a sauté pan and heating and tossing them together for a brief interlude before ladling the pasta into serving bowls. The noodles and the sauce get worked together for a second, turning them into a cohesive dish, not just noodles and a sauce. If you're making pasta for a big crowd, it's good to have a giant mixing bowl on hand for dressing pasta.

But that wasn't how pasta was served when we were growing up: it was pasta on a big platter, sauce over the top. Certain sauces still just seem right like that to us—like the Gnocchi Marinara with Fresh Ricotta (page 105) or Tony Durazzo's Spaghetti with Crabs (page 118). It's certainly the more traditional Italian-American approach. And though it's not how we plate the pastas at the restaurants, it is how we do it at home for some of these pastas, and we have noted so in those particular recipes.

FINISHING TOUCHES

Pasta without some kind of finish is either laziness or poverty incarnate, and only one of those is an acceptable excuse. Grated cheese is what we use most often. It adds fat, salt, and a little texture, and it helps to bind and thicken the sauce. Fresh herbs are different but just as good: they add contrast and brighten the dish. Dried bread crumbs (see page 13)—which you should always have on hand—add crunch and intrigue to a dish.

Rotary Cheese Grater

FRESH PASTA RECIPES

BASIC PASTA DOUGH

Makes 4 servings

2½ cups all-purpose flour

⅛ teaspoon fine sea salt

1 large egg

1 large egg yolk

½ cup water

1. Stir together the flour and salt in the bowl of a stand mixer. (To make pasta without a stand mixer, see the well method tutorial, illustrated on pages 96–97.) Add the egg, egg yolk, and water. Mix the dough with the dough hook, kneading it for 8 to 10 minutes, until it comes together in an integrated mass that clings to the hook. If the dough looks shaggy and dry, add more water by the tablespoon.

2. Remove the pasta dough from the bowl and knead it by hand on a lightly floured surface for a minute or so to bring it together and smooth it out. The resulting ball of dough should be smooth and resilient: it should spring back when poked. Wrap the dough in plastic wrap and let it rest for an hour or two (or as long as overnight) in the refrigerator.

3. Clamp the pasta machine onto the edge of your counter or work surface. Cut the ball of pasta dough into 3 pieces and lay a damp kitchen towel over them to keep them from drying out or forming a skin while you roll the dough into sheets. Use your hands to shape one piece of the pasta dough into a rough rectangle just wide and compact enough to fit through the rollers of the pasta machine. Roll the pasta through the widest setting six or seven times, folding it over end to end or creasing it down the middle after the first pass and cranking it through again. Don't add flour on the first four or five passes; you *want* the pasta to stick to itself during this stage to build up its strength, resilience, and eventual toothsomeness. By the fifth or sixth pass, you can dust it super-lightly with flour. After the seventh pass, it should be soft, with a nice sheen to it. Continue to crank the pasta through, narrowing the rollers with each pass. For fettuccine or tagliatelle, roll the pasta through all the way down to the thinnest setting. For linguine, stop a couple of degrees shy of that. Flour the sheet and put it under a damp kitchen towel until you are ready to cut it into noodles. Repeat with the remaining dough.

4. Dust each pasta sheet with flour before cutting it into the desired shape. For fettuccine, use the wider cutter on the pasta machine; for linguine, use the thinner one. For tagliatelle, lay the pasta sheets out on a cutting board and cut them into ½-inch-wide ribbons (don't worry if they're a little irregular). Dust the cut pasta lightly with flour, arrange on a baking sheet, preferably on a lightly floured piece of parchment, and cover with plastic wrap. Refrigerate until ready to cook.

5. To cook, drop the noodles into a large pot of boiling, well-salted water. Cook for about 2 minutes after the first few noodles begin to float on top of the water. Drain, toss with the sauce of your choice, and serve.

THE WELL METHOD

Falcinelli learned this technique from his dad while sitting on the bare, oil-spotted cement floor of the garage: you mix pasta dough the same way you mix concrete. So in case you think handmade noodles are something only grandmas can master, ask yourself this: is Grandma the only one who can pour a sidewalk?

1. Mound the flour in the middle of a nice big wooden cutting board, then burrow out a well—a crater, really—in the middle of the mountain.

Make the well.

2. Crack the eggs into a bowl and lightly beat them with a fork.
3. Add the water to the eggs, beat again, and then pour the egg mixture into the crater.

Add the beaten egg and water mixture.

4. Add the salt to the egg mixture.

5. Working in a steady, controlled, consistent, but gentle circular motion, use the fork to stir the eggs. The slow-motion egg eddy will draw in flour from the edges a little at a time—the idea is to slowly build a paste to create friction.

Add salt.   *Mix with a fork.*

6. At a certain point, the runny eggy part will turn into a sticky blob of dough encircled by a ring of flour. When that happens, retire the fork, flour your hands, and knead, pulling in flour as needed, for 8 minutes (set a timer), until the egg-filled flour volcano has been transformed into an elastic, resilient ball of dough. Wrap it in plastic until ready to roll it out as described in the Basic Pasta Dough recipe (page 94).

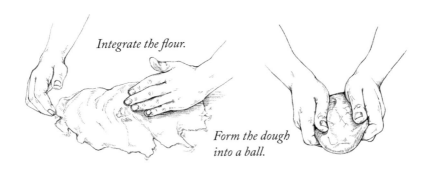

Integrate the flour.

Form the dough into a ball.

POTATO GNOCCHI

When we were opening the Spuntino, we asked Falcinelli's grandma Anne Martucci for her gnocchi recipe. She made the best. She was happy to roughly sketch it out for us over the phone. We took that information into the kitchen and gave it a shot. The resulting gnocchi were okay—good, even—but not exactly like hers.

Falcinelli dialed her up for a follow-up consultation, and that's when she realized we were honestly intending to serve her gnocchi at our restaurant. After that, she made every effort to communicate all the nuances of how she made them—like looking for the crystals as a sign the potatoes were perfectly cooked and giving the dough a good kneading, something that is rarely done with gnocchi in our experience.

And then, especially in the early days of the restaurant, she followed up on those lessons with frequent visits to the Spuntino—and she didn't hold back when we missed the mark and the gnocchi sucked. This recipe, which we've made about ten thousand times since our gnocchi finally got Anne's seal of approval, should save you from getting into that kind of trouble.

Makes enough for 6 servings

1½ pounds baking potatoes (3 good-sized potatoes)

½ teaspoon fine sea salt

1 large egg

¼ cup grated Pecorino Romano

1½ cups all-purpose flour, plus extra for shaping and dusting the pasta

1. Peel, quarter, and rinse the potatoes. Put them in a pot, add water to cover them by at least an inch, sprinkle in a large pinch of salt, and bring to a boil. Cook the potatoes until a thin-bladed knife meets little resistance when poked into them. (Falcinelli likes to use what we call "the crystal method." He says the potatoes are perfect when you crack one open with your fingers and it looks like it's dotted with tiny crystals.) Transfer the potatoes to a colander to drain and cover them with a dish towel to help them retain heat as they dry out a little bit.

2. When the potatoes are cool enough to handle but still warm, pass them through a food mill

or a ricer. (Lacking either, use a potato masher or a couple of forks with long tines to mash them, working them over evenly but not aggressively. You want crumbled potatoes, not potato paste.)

3. Combine the egg and cheese in the bowl of a stand mixer, add the potatoes and the flour, and work them together using the dough hook. Start slowly, then increase to medium speed. Knead the dough for 4 minutes, or until it comes together in a shaggy, integrated mass that clings to the hook.

4. Remove the dough from the mixer and knead it by hand on a floured surface for a couple of minutes to smooth it out. Cover it with a damp kitchen towel so it doesn't dry out as you work.

5. With floured hands (and with more flour close at hand, in case the dough gets sticky) grab a handball-sized piece of dough and roll it into a chubby cigar shape—thicker in the middle than at the ends. Then roll it into a snake ½ inch in diameter, working your palms from the middle out toward the ends. Cut the snake into gnocchi-sized pieces. (We use our thumbs to gauge how wide they should be.) Pinch each gnocchi and arrange on a baking sheet covered with parchment paper or a kitchen towel (to keep the pasta from sticking to the baking sheet). Repeat with the remaining dough. Use at once or hold the gnocchi in the refrigerator for a few hours.

6. To cook, drop the gnocchi into a large pot of boiling, well-salted water and cook for 2 minutes after the first few begin to float on top of the water. Drain, sauce, and serve.

RICOTTA CAVATELLI

Castronovo's great-grandma Carmella used to make cavatelli. She used a flour-and-water dough and shaped them by hand—crimping a pinch of dough into the proper folded-over, wormlike shape, then rolling it over the tines of a fork to mark it with sauce-thirsty grooves. It was an afternoon-long labor of love, so it was a special treat, an occasional thing.

That was because Carmella didn't have a cavatelli maker. These machines turn making cavatelli from the chore it was for her into fresh pasta that can be made from scratch and on the table in about an hour—honest.

Makes enough for
6 servings

4 cups all-purpose flour, plus extra for dusting the pasta

1 pound (about 1 pint) ricotta

1 large egg

Pinch of fine sea salt

Up to ¼ cup milk or water if necessary to adjust the dough

1. Combine the flour, cheese, egg, and salt in the bowl of a stand mixer fitted with the dough hook and knead on medium speed until the dough comes together in a shaggy, integrated mass that clings to the hook. If the dough looks dry and refuses to coalesce into a ball, add milk by the tablespoon to encourage it. Remove the dough from the mixer and knead it by hand for a couple of minutes to smooth it out. Or, if you don't have a mixer, use the well method described on pages 96–97, mixing together the egg and ricotta (instead of the egg and water) and plopping that down in the center of the well. Otherwise, it works the same way.

2. Clamp the cavatelli maker onto the edge of the counter or work surface. Cut the ball of dough into 4 equal pieces. Roll each ball into a snake just less than 1 inch thick. Crank the snakes through the cavatelli machine, lightly dust the cavatelli with flour, and arrange on a baking sheet. Use at once or hold for up to 1 day in the fridge.

3. To cook, drop the cavatelli into a large pot of well-salted boiling water and cook for 4 minutes after the first few begin to float on top of the water. Drain, sauce, and serve.

CAVATELLI WITH SAUSAGE & BROWNED SAGE BUTTER

This is one of our most popular dishes. It's renowned as a hangover curative among the people we work with and the 10-to-1 favorite for what a guy will order on a first date. (His date will almost always order the Sweet Potato Ravioli in Cheese Broth on page 110. It just works out that way.)

Two small but important notes on this otherwise very easy recipe: the sausage must be precooked so it can be cut into coins; cutting it into coins is advantageous because sliced sausage has more surface area to brown, and browned sausage is better. Also, the sauce is *browned* butter. It's a stage of doneness, something we were taught in cooking school: *beurre noisette.* It should be visibly browned, with a hazelnut-like aroma. Don't skimp on the browning.

At the restaurant we bake the sausages ahead of time, but simmering the sausage, as in this recipe, is faster when you're cooking for just a few people. If you're making cavatelli for a crowd, cook a baking sheet's worth— probably 3 or 4 pounds of sausage—by lining the links up on the baking sheet, adding a good splash of water, and baking them at 350°F until they're cooked through, about 30 minutes. Slice the cooked sausages into coins and proceed with Step 3.

1. Put a large pot of water on to boil and salt it well.

2. Meanwhile, put the sausages into your widest sauté pan with ½ inch of water and turn the heat to medium. After 10 minutes, flip the sausages over and simmer them for another 5 minutes (replenish the water if it threatens to boil off). After 15 minutes, the sausages should be firm and cooked through. Remove the sausages to a cutting board (discard the water) and slice them into coins just shy of ½ inch. (You can do this an hour or even a day ahead of time if you like.)

3. Add 1 tablespoon of the butter to the pan and turn the heat to medium-high. After a minute, add the sausage coins in an even layer and let them cook, untouched, unstirred, unfussed with, until they're deeply browned on the first side. (If there's not enough room to brown all the sausage in one pan—which there will very probably not be—split it between two pans or brown it in two batches and use an additional tablespoon of butter.) Flip and brown them on the B side. The browning is integral to the ultimate depth of flavor of the finished dish—don't stint on it. When the sausage is browned, remove it from the pan (a plate lined with paper towels is a nice place to hold it) and return the pan to the burner.

4. Keep the heat at medium-high and add the sage, the remaining 6 tablespoons of butter, and a few twists of white pepper. Stir the butter and scrape at the browned bits on the bottom of the pan with a wooden spoon. After a minute or two, it should stop foaming and

Serves 6

1 pound hot Italian pork sausage (4 to 6 links, depending on the size of the sausage)

7 tablespoons unsalted butter

8 to 10 sage leaves (fewer if they are very large, more if they are very small)

Freshly ground white pepper

Ricotta Cavatelli (page 100)

1 cup grated Pecorino Romano

½ cup flat-leaf parsley leaves, coarsely chopped

start to take on color. That's when you should drop the ricotta cavatelli into the boiling water. Continue to cook the butter until it's deeply browned and fragrant, about 4 minutes more, which should be just about how long the cavatelli takes to cook.

5. Do not drain the cavatelli too thoroughly. The water clinging to the pasta will give the sauce body. Add it to the butter sauce along with the sausage and stir.

6. Add the cheese, stir again, and portion the cavatelli among serving plates. Scatter each with a couple of pinches of parsley. Serve immediately.

GNOCCHI MARINARA WITH FRESH RICOTTA

This tomato-and-ricotta treatment is the classic. Mix it up by swapping the cavatelli for the gnocchi in this recipe and the gnocchi for the cavatelli in Cavatelli with Sausage & Browned Sage Butter on page 102.

1. Put a large pot of water on to boil and salt it well.

2. Warm the tomato sauce in a saucepan.

3. Cook the gnocchi in the boiling salted water, about 4 minutes. Drain well and portion them out among six serving bowls. Top each portion with ½ cup of the sauce and then with a couple of tablespoons of grated cheese and a large dollop of fresh ricotta. Serve immediately.

Serves 6

3 cups Tomato Sauce (page xx)

Potato Gnocchi (page 98)

½ cup grated Pecorino Romano

1 cup fresh ricotta

Linguine with Fava Beans, Garlic, Tomato & Bread Crumbs

In the spring, right after asparagus shows up at the market, fava beans arrive—one of the first encouraging signs that the root-vegetable tyranny of New York's winter is over and there will actually be fresh stuff around again. This pasta was born around that time a few years ago—vegetables back in season, summer looming, the need to get fit asserting itself. So it's favas, tomato sauce (because, left to our own devices, we'd put tomato sauce in everything), and bread crumbs to finish it, to add a little textural intrigue. A perfect spring-into-summer pasta.

SHUCKING FAVA BEANS

Shucking favas is as easy as can be, but it's a time-eating chore. As such, do your best to farm it out to unsuspecting friends or relatives who ask if there's anything they can help with.

Put a large pot of water on to boil and salt it well. While the water's coming to a boil, string the pods and pull them apart. Pop out the pale green beans. Discard the pods.

Prepare an ice water bath.

Blanch the fava beans for 10 seconds in the boiling water and immediately remove them to the water bath to cool; drain. Pinch the beans between your fingers to squeeze the bright green inner beans from their pale green skins.

You can shuck fava beans up to a day in advance and store them, covered, in the refrigerator until you're ready to use them.

1. Put a large pot of water on to boil and salt it well.

2. Meanwhile, heat the grapeseed oil over high heat. After a minute, add the garlic. Cook it, stirring occasionally, for a minute or two, just until it is fragrant. Add the favas and stir or toss to coat them in the oil. After 30 seconds, add the vegetable broth (carefully, in one big addition) to cool the pan down. Stir or shake the pan, then wait for the broth to come to a boil and add the tomato sauce, a teaspoon of salt, and the red pepper flakes. Drop the pasta into the boiling water to cook and add the butter to the sauce.

3. Drain the pasta and add it to the warm sauce. Turn off the heat and toss the pasta to coat it in the sauce. Portion the pasta among serving bowls and garnish with the olive oil, grated cheese, and bread crumbs. Offer black pepper at the table.

Serves 4

Fine sea salt

¼ cup grapeseed oil

4 cloves garlic, smashed and roughly chopped

1 cup shucked favas (from about 3 pounds of whole beans), blanched and peeled (see box opposite)

1 cup Vegetable Broth (page 14)

1 cup Tomato Sauce (page xx)

Large pinch of red pepper flakes

Basic Pasta Dough (page 94), cut into linguine

2 tablespoons unsalted butter

¼ cup olive oil

4 teaspoons grated Pecorino Romano

4 heaping teaspoons dried bread crumbs

Freshly ground black pepper

Linguine Cacio e Pepe

The first time we went to Sicily to visit Tommaso, our olive oil guy, we got in late. It was nearly 10 P.M. by the time we made it to Partanna. We were hungry and tired, and when Tommaso caught sight of us, he told us he knew just what we needed: pasta cacio e pepe, pasta with Pecorino cheese and black pepper. He took us to a little mom-and-pop place and ordered a round for the table. He was right: It was comforting, like the buttered noodles everybody's mom makes for them as kids. And it was so simple and economical, we knew it would be perfect for the Spuntino.

But when we got back to Brooklyn, we got caught up in catching up and never quite got around to putting it on the menu. That is, not until Tommaso came to New York, showing up late at night after a long flight, and asked where the cacio e pepe was. Castronovo had to hop into the kitchen and make him a plate. After a couple of days of tweaking the formula, it went on the menu.

1. Put a large pot of water on to boil and salt it well.

2. Combine the cheese broth, salt, black pepper, red pepper flakes, and ½ cup of the Pecorino Romano in a wide saucepan over medium heat. Bring the contents of the pan to a near-simmer. It should be milky and melding together but not bubbling or boiling. When the cheese melts and the sauce thickens, drop the pasta into the boiling water. The dish is almost done.

3. Drain the pasta well and add it to the sauce. Add the olive oil and butter and toss until the butter is melted and the pasta is coated and glossy.

4. Portion the pasta among four serving plates and garnish each with a tablespoon of the remaining Pecorino Romano. Pass black pepper at the table.

Serves 4

1 teaspoon fine sea salt

2 cups Cheese Broth (page 14)

4 teaspoons medium-coarse black pepper, plus more for serving

1 teaspoon red pepper flakes

¾ cup grated Pecorino Romano

Basic Pasta Dough (page 94), cut into linguine

¼ cup olive oil

4 tablespoons unsalted butter

Freshly ground black pepper

SWEET POTATO RAVIOLI IN CHEESE BROTH

Chinese five-spice powder, wonton skins, and scallions: You might get the impression that this dish is half Chinese. It's not, it's just that five-spice is the perfect sweet-spicy complement to sweet potatoes; wonton wrappers are the easiest, most surefire, and low-waste way to make ravioli (and that's coming from guys who have absolutely no problem whipping up a batch of fresh pasta dough); and scallions, well, scallions are good on everything. Plus, come on—the Chinese gave the Italians noodles to turn into pasta and the water buffalo that make the best mozzarella. What's wrong with borrowing a few more things?

Serves 8

3 large sweet potatoes, scrubbed

A negligible amount of olive oil

Fine sea salt and freshly ground white pepper

2 tablespoons honey

¼ teaspoon Chinese five-spice powder

48 round wonton wrappers

4 tablespoons unsalted butter

1. Heat the oven to 350°F. Slick the potatoes with oil, sprinkle with salt and white pepper, and wrap individually in aluminum foil. Bake for 1 hour, or until very tender.

2. Halve the sweet potatoes and scoop the flesh into a mixing bowl. Add the honey, five-spice powder, and a large pinch of salt. Stir to combine, then taste and adjust as needed. Let it cool down a little.

3. Prep your pasta-making station: the bowl of ravioli filling, the pile of wonton wrappers, a cutting board to work on, a small bowl of water (to seal the ravioli), and a baking sheet lined with parchment paper or plastic wrap. Put a teaspoon of filling into the center of a wonton skin, dip your finger in the bowl of water and use it to wet the rim of the wonton skin, then fold the wrapper closed, pinching the edges to

seal. Lay the ravioli on the baking sheet and repeat until they are all stuffed. The ravioli can be used right away or frozen on the baking sheet. (Once they have frozen solid, transfer them to a freezer bag or other container and store for up to a month.)

4. When you're ready to cook and serve, put a large pot of water on to boil and salt it well.

5. Melt the butter in a wide saucepan over medium heat. Add the sage leaves and cook them for a minute or so, just until aromatic. Add the cheese broth, season it with a pinch of salt and a few turns of white pepper, and bring to a simmer.

6. Drop the ravioli into the pot of salted water; they should bob to the surface of the pot in about 3 minutes. Remove the ravioli from the water and divide among the serving bowls. Ladle a cup or so of the broth into each bowl, and garnish with a scattering of scallions.

5 or 6 sage leaves

8 cups Cheese Broth (page 14)

4 scallions, white and very light green parts only, cut into long, fine julienne

Linguine with Garlic & Frankies Olive Oil

This pasta is fast, nourishing, and easily made when you have very little on hand. If you're using fresh pasta, you can make the sauce and cook the pasta in just about the same amount of time. If you're using dried pasta, you should drop the pasta in boiling water, wait 3 or 4 minutes, and then start the sauce. Either way, you'll spend longer getting the water to boil than you will cooking.

Serves 4

1 cup olive oil

4 cloves garlic, smashed and chopped

1 cup Vegetable Broth (page 14) or water

¼ cup chopped flat-leaf parsley

Basic Pasta Dough (page 94), cut into linguine, or 1 pound dried linguine

½ cup grated Pecorino Romano

1. Put a large pot of water on to boil and salt it well.

2. Meanwhile, choose a big, wide pan. A sauté pan is ideal—something with high sides to hold all the pasta when you add it to the sauce, so it can drink it all up. Pour half the oil into the pan, put the pan on the burner, and turn the heat to medium-high. After a minute or so, add the garlic. Cook the garlic, shaking the pan or stirring intermittently, until it's taking on a little bit of golden color and is notably fragrant—intensifying, sharpening, asserting itself but not veering into acrid, overtly sharp territory—2 to 3 minutes, not much more.

3. When the garlic is there, add the broth, parsley, and the remaining olive oil to the pan and stir or swirl until the sauce starts to emulsify. Time the cooking of the pasta so it's ready a minute or so after the garlic; then add it to the pan, not taking too much care to drain it. Toss it thoroughly in the pan until it's glossy with sauce. Portion the pasta among serving bowls, finish each with a couple of tablespoons of Pecorino Romano, and serve immediately. You probably want to bring the bottle of olive oil to the table with you in case anybody wants some extra.

TAGLIATELLE WITH BRAISED LAMB RAGU

There's nothing traditional about this dish. It's a French-style braised lamb shoulder pulled apart and then thrown together with the obligatory Italian-American addition of tomato sauce, tossed with pasta, and finished with fresh tarragon, an herb that's typically more at home with seafood and white sauces.

It is a two-day dish: the lamb gets braised on day one, and you make the sauce and pasta and put the dish together on day two. (Actually, if you make it the way we make it, it can be a three-day dish, since you need the veal stock to braise the lamb. But you can make that and freeze it weeks in advance.)

We like a two-day braise for two reasons: it's a mellower schedule to cook on, and if you fully chill down the braising liquid, it is easier to degrease it completely and replace the cooked fat with fresher fat, like olive oil or butter, which is better tasting and easier to eat.

The first step of braising is browning. You can brown the meat on the stovetop, but even if takes a smidge longer, we brown our meat in the oven because it's more contained—i.e., there's not a cloud of meat smoke billowing from a sauté pan. The next thing to pay attention to is what you're braising the meat in. The ideal braising liquid is veal stock. If you're skipping that, use water, not that canned stock crap, and add veal or beef bones when you braise the meat to help make up the difference.

Although you can substitute basil or mint for the tarragon, it's really not the same (we've tried every variation). There's something about the tarragon that mellows and tames the lamb, and something about it that makes the whole thing take off.

Serves 8

DAY 1

1 piece bone-in lamb shoulder (about 3 pounds)

Fine sea salt

Freshly ground black pepper

1 tablespoon grapeseed oil

1 medium yellow onion, chopped

1 large carrot, chopped

2 stalks celery, chopped

½ cup chopped fennel (just the outer tougher layers or as much as half of a small bulb, chopped)

½ cup, or a close approximation, parsley stems

3 plum tomatoes

6 cups Veal Stock (page 145) or, failing that, 2 pounds or so beef or veal bones (knuckle, marrow, doesn't matter) and 6 cups water

DAY 1

TIME TO BRAISE THE LAMB

The ideal cut for this braise is a bone-in lamb shoulder. If you can't find one—if the butcher only has tied-up boneless shoulder, that's fine; just augment it by buying a pound or so of bones (anything—a couple of marrow bones, a veal shin, a lamb shank) and cook them alongside the meat.

———————⋙✦⋘———————

1. Heat the oven to 450°F. Season the lamb generously with salt and pepper. Put it on a baking sheet and pop it into the oven. (If you are using bones in place of stock, they should be roasted alongside the meat and then discarded after the meat's been braised.) Roast the lamb until the exterior is deeply browned, about 45 minutes; flip it once mid-roast if you think of it. Remove the lamb to a platter to rest. Turn the oven down to 300°F.

2. While the lamb is roasting, heat the grapeseed oil in your widest skillet or sauté pan over high heat for 1 minute, then add the onion, carrot, celery, and fennel and turn the heat down to medium-high. Add a large pinch of salt and sauté until the mass of vegetables has shrunk and begun to take on a golden caramel color and is browning in spots, about 20 minutes. Remove from the heat.

3. Put the lamb shoulder in a 6- or 8-quart heavy-bottomed ovenproof pot—something that will hold it, the aromatics, and the stock snugly. Add the cooked vegetables and parsley stems. Crush the tomatoes with your hands

right over the pot and nestle them into it. Add the stock; it should nearly but not quite cover the meat. Cover the pot, pop it into the oven, and braise the lamb for 2 hours—at which point the meat should yield uncomplainingly to the tugging of a fork.

4. Remove the meat from the stock and let it rest and regain its composure. Strain the stock into a container (or two), lightly pressing on the vegetables in the strainer to wring out any flavor left in them. Discard the spent vegetables and parsley stems. Cover and refrigerate the broth.

5. Use two forks to pull the lamb apart into fine ropy shreds, as you would for pulled pork. Discard any big chunks of gristle or fat (or save them for your dog), pack the pulled meat into a bowl or other container, cover it, and put it in the fridge.

Day 2
TIME TO EAT

1. Remove the stock from the refrigerator and skin/scrape off the pale, hardened layer of fat that has formed on its surface. Put it in a largish braising pot, maybe the same one you braised the shoulder in. Add the tomato sauce (or tomatoes), put the pot over medium-high heat, and simmer the broth and tomato sauce for 15 minutes, so they get a chance to know each other. (If you're substituting canned tomatoes, give them 30 to 45 minutes with the broth.) Put a large pot of water (for the pasta) on the stove to boil and salt it well.

DAY 2

4 cups lamb stock from Day 1

4 cups Tomato Sauce (page xx) or one 28-ounce can plus one 10-ounce can tomatoes, crushed by hand

Braised lamb from Day 1

Fine sea salt

(ingredients continued on next page)

A double recipe of Basic Pasta Dough (page 94), cut into tagliatelle

½ cup chopped flat-leaf parsley

8 tablespoons (1 stick) unsalted butter

½ teaspoon freshly ground white pepper

⅓ cup chopped tarragon for garnish

Olive oil for drizzling

2. Add the lamb to the sauce and stir to distribute it well. Warm it for 5 to 10 minutes, or just until it's heated through. (If you're going to reserve some of the sauce to freeze it, now's the time. Adjust your deployment of butter, herbs, and seasoning accordingly.)

3. Cook the pasta; it might be best to cook it in two shifts.

4. While the pasta is boiling, raise the heat under the ragu to high and add the parsley, butter, ½ teaspoon salt, and white pepper. Stir to distribute the flavors and ensure the butter melts. Taste the sauce and add more salt if needed.

5. When the pasta's ready, drain and add to the pot of lamb sauce. Stir well and let sit for a minute or so in the sauce to soak up some flavor.

6. Portion the pasta among individual plates or mound it on a serving platter. Shower it with the fresh tarragon, splash on some olive oil, and serve.

DRIED PASTA RECIPES

ORECCHIETTE WITH PISTACHIOS

This pasta sauce is what we think of in the States as a pesto, but with the ratio of nuts to herbs flipflopped. The main ingredients are Sicilian in emphasis: the Sicilian pistachios, which are incredibly sweet and fruity, not like the cheap ones we eat in front of the TV here; and some mint, which reflects the North African influence on Sicilian cuisine.

Serves 4

Fine sea salt

1½ cups shelled unsalted green pistachios, preferably Sicilian

1 clove minced garlic

2 tablespoons finely chopped mint

½ cup extra virgin olive oil, plus extra for serving

½ cup grated Pecorino Romano

1 pound orecchiette

4 scallions, white and light green parts only, julienned long and fine

1. Put a large pot of water on to boil and salt it well.

2. Meanwhile, roughly chop the pistachios by hand or in a food processor. Toss the pistachios with the garlic, mint, and olive oil in a small mixing bowl. Add the cheese and a large pinch of salt and stir to combine.

3. Cook the pasta in the boiling water until al dente, following the package directions. Drain, reserving ½ cup of the pasta cooking water, and return the pasta to the pot over low heat.

4. Add the pesto to the pot, along with the reserved pasta cooking water, and heat, tossing constantly, until the orecchiette are coated with the sauce. Transfer to bowls or a serving platter, garnish with the scallions, and serve, passing additional olive oil at the table.

Tony Durazzo's Spaghetti with Crabs

Every summer, once the season really settles in, something triggers it: one of us sees a basket of crabs at a fish market or blue claw crabs on a menu at another restaurant. Regardless of what sets us off, all of sudden it's like, "Hey, time to put the crab pasta on for a couple of weeks. Somebody go pick up a bushel." It's gotten to the point where it's not quite summer if we haven't eaten our way through a half-dozen orders of crab pasta.

The Spuntino spaghetti with crabs is a riff on our friend Tony Durazzo's recipe, a dish his mom served him growing up.

When we first started making crab pasta, we used fresh pasta; we picked the meat out of the cooked crabs and garnished the finished dish with it. Tony's version is a big platter of boiled spaghetti with crabmeat-infused tomato sauce poured over the top and the simmered crabs in a bowl on the side.

While we were testing recipes for this book, we got together with Tony and made the Spuntino-style and Tony-style versions side by side. Tony's idea of dried pasta is just right for this dish—better than fresh even, so don't go to the extra trouble. And when we were standing around in the kitchen making a platter of the pasta for just a few of us, that step of removing the meat from the shells felt a little prissy, like a little bit too much work. So we're also deferring to Tony's predilection for serving the cooked crabs on the side of the pasta, which is one of those ingenious classic Italian-American tricks: you get the rich, crabby tomato sauce on the pasta and, from the same cooking process, the bowl of cooked crabs. Two dishes out of one!

Italians are great at turning eight blue crabs into a feast. It's imperative to have good bread on hand when making this dish. Once the pasta and crabs are gone, you'll need it to sop up the leftover sauce.

1. Heat the olive oil in a wide, deep pot over medium-high heat. After a minute or so, add the garlic and cook it for a minute or two, just until it's fragrant. Add the crushed tomatoes, parsley, and red pepper flakes, stir well, and bring to a simmer. Let the sauce cook while you clean the crabs.

2. Turn the heat under the pot up to high, add the crabs, and wait for the sauce to come to a boil. When it does, turn the heat down, medium to medium low, so the sauce simmers gently. After 30 minutes or so, remove the crabs from the tomato sauce and put them in a large, deep serving bowl. Cover to keep warm.

3. Meanwhile, put a large pot of water on to boil and salt it well.

4. Drop the pasta into the boiling water and cook it for a minute less than its package directs: crab sauce likes extra–al dente pasta. Drain the pasta.

5. Put the pasta on a large serving platter and dress it with a generous hit of olive oil and a sprinkle of salt. Pour the sauce over the pasta. Tear the basil leaves in halves or thirds and scatter them over the pasta. Season it with as much black pepper as you can stand. Serve the crabs on the side of the pasta (with another bowl for the shells and have plenty of napkins around.

Serves 8

¼ cup olive oil, plus more to finish the dish

3 cloves garlic, smashed and roughly chopped

Two 28-ounce cans San Marzano tomatoes, crushed by hand, or 8 cups Tomato Sauce (page xx)

¼ cup chopped flat-leaf parsley

Large pinch (or two) of red pepper flakes

8 meaty blue crabs

Fine sea salt

2 pounds spaghetti

1 cup fresh basil leaves

Freshly ground black pepper

TONY DURAZZO

COOKING WITH TONY

"You want the dish to be oily," says Tony, pouring oil into the pan. Taking his pronouncement as a cue to extrapolate, he continues, "You know what I say? When you're eating the crabs, the oil should be dripping down to your ELBOWS!" *He tilts his head, his eyes looking over the top of his glasses, and arches his eyebrows to add emphasis.*

"The important thing with the sauce is the tomatoes should be lumpy. You wanna crush the tomatoes with your hands." Brief pause to squeeze a tomato. "The sauce should be soupy." Tomato juice squirts onto Tony's shirt. The dish goes on.

"Bring it to a boil, turn it down so it . . ." He means to say simmers, *but he trails off. "That's it. The rest is watching it cook." A smile.*

"Look at this," Tony calls out, an accusatory finger pointed at the sauce pot. "When it starts to put up that pink-red crab stuff . . . foam . . . it's time to drop the pasta."

Falcinelli interjects, calling the foam "impurities from the crab." He says it should be skimmed, but nobody goes running for a ladle.

The pasta, drained, goes on a platter, grandma-style, then Tony dumps the tomato sauce over it. The crushed tomatoes congregate on top of the pasta; the juices drain through to the plate. Tony lifts up some of the pasta and says, "See, the sauce should be soupy underneath."

Basil leaves torn into uneven rags are scattered over the pasta. Tony grinds black pepper over the platter until he's tired of tweaking the grinder. Time to eat.

> ***VARIATION**—In the not entirely unlikely event that you are unable to find blue crabs, don't fret. Frozen Alaskan king crab legs know no season and are a perfectly good substitute. Figure on about 2 pounds of frozen crab legs for 8 people and shorten the simmering time to 20 minutes. You may want to use the back of a heavy knife to crack open the sturdier legs before serving them or just tell your family to use their teeth.*

Frank Falcinelli (left) and Frank Castronovo, in Sicily's Belice Valley, near Partanna, Italy. The grove of Nocellara olive trees in which they are standing is the source of their house brand of olive oil.

Frank Falcinelli, 1989

Frank Castronovo
(with Paul Bocuse), 1991

Frankies 457 Court Street Spuntino in Carroll Gardens, Brooklyn

Frankies 17 Clinton Street Spuntino on the Lower East Side

The garden at Frankies in Brooklyn with the F train zipping by in the distance.

Take it outside in the summer:
See our ideas for Summertime
Grilling on pages 183–87.

Patronize butchers, delis, cheese shops, and wine stores where you can talk to the people behind the counter. We prefer neighborhood places—like Paisanos on Smith Street in Brooklyn (pictured here)—where the deli cases are older than we are. There are still plenty of shops like this around the country, and

Antipasto—whether it's a full spread or just a bowl of olives—is the way we like to start a meal at the Spuntino. See the chapter starting on page 25 to get going.

Simply roasted vegetables (see pages 34–45) are great on their own and even better when mixed together in our Roasted Vegetable Salad (page 72).

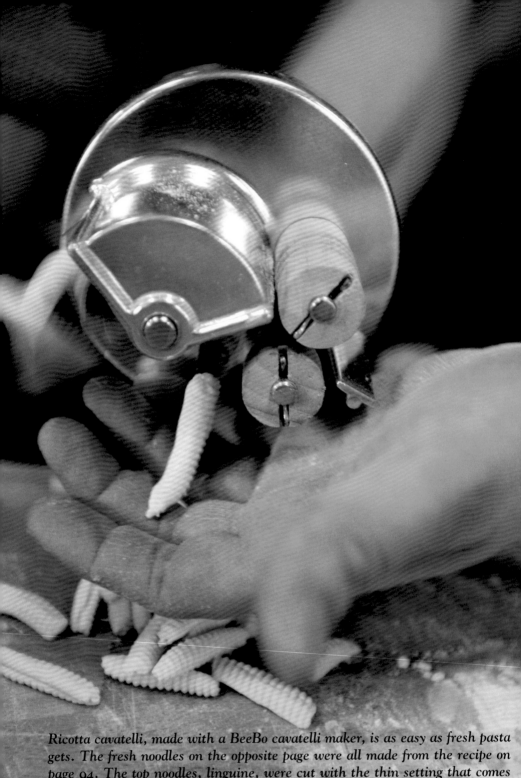

Ricotta cavatelli, made with a BeeBo cavatelli maker, is as easy as fresh pasta gets. The fresh noodles on the opposite page were all made from the recipe on page 94. The top noodles, linguine, were cut with the thin setting that comes with a pasta machine; the spaghetti in the middle was cut with an attachment that typically is sold separately; the tagliatelle noodles on the bottom were sliced by hand.

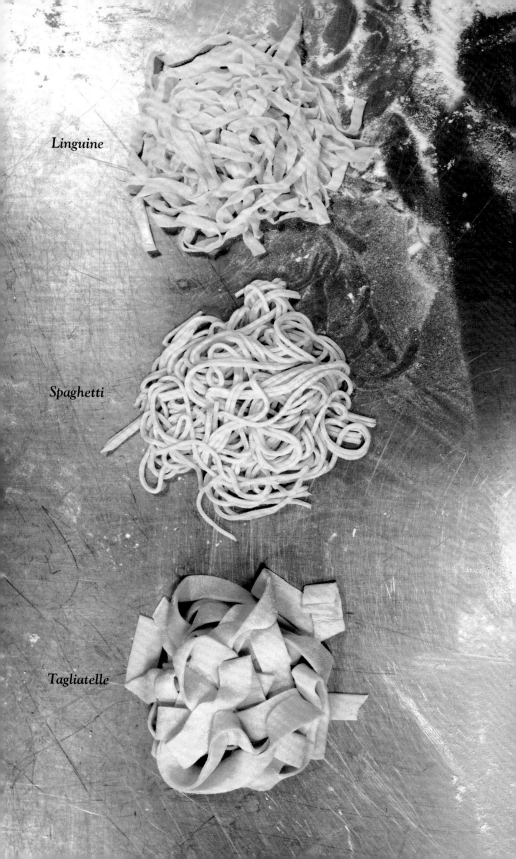

Linguine

Spaghetti

Tagliatelle

Luis "Luigi" Espinosa preparing Linguine with Fava Beans, Garlic, Tomato & Bread Crumbs (page 106).

The Sunday Sauce in progress: after your garlic is good and golden, get the tomatoes in the pot and simmer, simmer, simmer until it's time to eat.

Meatballs (page 124) in the making . . .

. . . Meatballs ready to meet their maker.

CHAPTER 6

MEATS &
OTHER MAIN COURSES

Meatball (actual size)

When we're cooking at home, we like putting the pasta course together as the last big gasp of effort of the evening. If there will be more food to follow, we like to have the work done ahead of time. Our approach isn't any different at the Spuntino. All of these dishes can be made mostly in advance.

And we know as well as you do that when you can get the worrying and working done way in advance, it lets the meal and everything that really needs to be enjoyed—like your family's or guests' company—command the center of your attention.

MEATBALLS

In 1993, Falcinelli was working as a "consulting chef"—kind of like a utility infielder—for a U.S.-based restaurant group. He was dispatched to the Grand Amsterdam Hotel in Holland, where his job was to assist one of the group's chefs, Don Pintabona of the Tribeca Grill, prepare a special week of all-American dinners.

When Falcinelli was informed that Don was bringing an additional helper, he expected some young gun—a hotshot who could really bang out the food. Instead, he discovered that the chef had brought along a friend, a guy in his late forties with big thick glasses, a beard, and a shock of gray hair: Tony Durazzo. On first meeting, Tony told Frank, "I'm not a cook." It was only partly the truth.

Because even if Tony wasn't a restaurant professional (he was actually a trained draftsman), he knew what he was doing well enough. Frank took the lead on the cooking; Tony on the storytelling. Tony was born in Naples and raised in Carroll Gardens, Brooklyn. He used to sneak into the Fillmore East back in the 1960s and hitchhiked from coast to coast in the 1970s. He had a million stories to tell, and it turned out he and Frank lived right around the corner from each other in the West Village.

Tony told Frank all about his family's food, about the way they cooked, and about how they made the best meatballs. If you grow up around Italians, you know that most talk like that is bluster. But Tony seemed to know what he was talking about.

Shortly thereafter, back in New York, Tony fried up a batch of his meatballs and walked them downstairs and around the corner from his place on Morton Street to Falcinelli's apartment on Commerce Street. When he arrived, the meatballs were still warm. They weren't in a sauce, just loose in a baking pan, topped with grated parmesan that had largely fallen off during the trip around the corner.

Falcinelli didn't think they were good—he thought they were great. They reminded him of the meatballs he was raised on, but Tony's addition of pine nuts and raisins—which added texture and sweetness—pushed them to the next level.

The two talked about setting up a food cart or a restaurant based on Tony's recipe. They had a good laugh about it: a meatball restaurant! They laughed about it until they laughed it off. Falcinelli put it way back on one of the backburners of his mind, next to a million other schemes that would probably never see the light. But a decade later, the seeds of this particular plan—those meatballs—grew into the Spuntino.

Note that Tony fries his meatballs and we bake ours. Both recipes are here for your meatball-making pleasure. Please also note that ground beef for meatballs should clock in at around 10% fat (or 90% lean). Meat that's too fatty makes for flabby, greasy meatballs.

*Makes 6 servings;
18 to 20 meatballs*

**4 slices bread
(2 packed cups'
worth)**

**2 pounds
ground beef**

**3 cloves garlic,
minced**

**¼ cup finely
chopped flat-
leaf parsley**

**¼ cup grated
Pecorino Romano,
plus about 1 cup
for serving**

¼ cup raisins

¼ cup pine nuts

**1½ teaspoons
fine sea salt**

**15 turns
white pepper**

4 large eggs

**½ cup dried
bread crumbs**

**Tomato Sauce
(page xx)**

THE SPUNTINO WAY

1. Heat the oven to 325°F. Put the fresh bread in a bowl, cover it with water, and let it soak for a minute or so. Pour off the water and wring out the bread, then crumble and tear it into tiny pieces.

2. Combine the bread with all the remaining ingredients except the tomato sauce in a medium mixing bowl, adding them in the order they are listed. Add the dried bread crumbs last to adjust for wetness: the mixture should be moist wet, not sloppy wet.

3. Shape the meat mixture into handball-sized meatballs and space them evenly on a baking sheet. Bake for 25 to 30 minutes. The meatballs will be firm but still juicy and gently yielding when they're cooked through. (At this point, you can cool the meatballs and hold them in the refrigerator for as long as a couple of days or freeze them for the future.)

4. Meanwhile, heat the tomato sauce in a sauté pan large enough to accommodate the meatballs comfortably.

5. Dump the meatballs into the pan of sauce and nudge the heat up ever so slightly. Simmer the meatballs for half an hour or so (this isn't one of those cases where longer is better) so they can soak up some sauce. Keep them there until it's time to eat.

6. Serve the meatballs 3 to a person in a healthy helping of the red sauce, and hit everybody's portion—never the pan—with a fluffy mountain of grated cheese. Reserve the leftover tomato sauce (it will be super-extra-delicious) and use it anywhere tomato sauce is called for in this book.

TONY'S WAY

You'll need a few cups of oil for this method—enough so it's about ½ inch deep in the pan you use to fry the meatballs. We like to use a 50/50 mix of olive oil and grapeseed oil. And Tony uses Parmigiano-Reggiano instead of Pecorino Romano, which is not a bad move at all.

1. Make the meatball mixture as directed in Step 2 on page 126, substituting Parmigiano for the Pecorino, then shape the meat mixture into golf-ball-sized meatballs.

2. Combine the olive and grapeseed oils in a large sauté pan or skillet over medium heat. When the oil is hot but not smoking (a pinch of meatball mix should sizzle excitedly when dropped into the oil), add the meatballs. You'll probably want to fry them in two batches, so as not to overcrowd the pan. Fry them, flipping them over occasionally, until they're browned and cooked through, 10 to 12 minutes per batch. Use a slotted spoon to transfer the meatballs to a plate lined with paper towels to drain briefly.

3. Meanwhile, heat the tomato sauce in a sauté pan large enough to hold the meatballs.

4. After they've had a chance to towel off, put the meatballs into the tomato sauce hot tub. Let them hang out in there for about 30 minutes before you unleash them on your friends, blanketed generously with freshly grated Parmesan cheese.

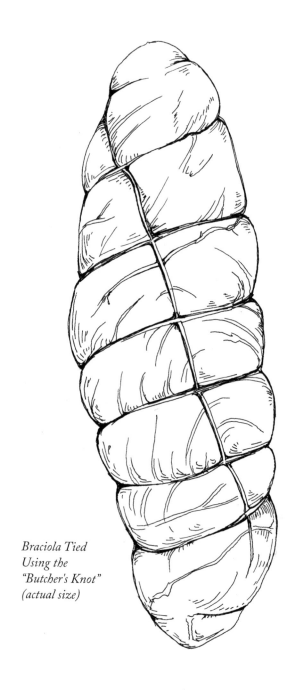

Braciola Tied
Using the
"Butcher's Knot"
(actual size)

PORK BRACIOLA MARINARA

First things first: it's pronounced bra-JOEL (and that's pronouncing *Joel* like a French name, with a soft "j"). It's always painful to hear somebody order brock-ee-O-la.

Having braciola on the menu brings a lot of real Italians (and by that we mean died-in-the-wool Italian Americans, not people from Italy) into the restaurant. They want to check out your braciola, to see if it's up to snuff. Anybody who grew up with this food never gets tired of eating it . . . or judging it. And while a dyspeptic minority can't ever get over their mom's cooking, most people who come in looking to check out our braciola generally seem to like it. We know because they tell us it is just like theirs.

Something to know: Braciola is the secret of an epic tomato sauce. It was always simmering away in the Sunday sauces of our youth (see page 151). That pork/provolone/tomato combination is just impossible to beat. Yeah, people will tell you beef braciola is really great and all that, but it's always drier. It's better as a leftover, thinly sliced and stuffed into a sandwich. But pork, and the tomato sauce that the pork creates, is the best.

Serves 6

Six ½-inch-thick boneless pork shoulder steaks (8 ounces each)

Fine sea salt and freshly ground white pepper

1 clove, garlic, minced

⅔ cup chopped flat-leaf parsley

1 cup grated aged provolone

1 cup freshly grated Parmesan, plus more for serving

1 recipe Tomato Sauce (page xx)

1. Butterfly the pork: With the palm of one hand firmly steadying a cutlet on the cutting board, and with your knife blade parallel to the meat, slice almost all the way through the meat, leaving the last ¼ inch uncut.

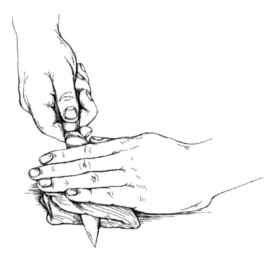

2. Open up the cutlet like a book, season it with salt and white pepper, and set it aside. Repeat with the remaining pieces of pork.

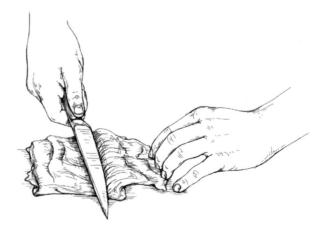

3. Sprinkle the cut side of one cutlet with a tiny pinch of minced garlic, a couple of pinches of parsley, and a generous tablespoon of each cheese.

4. Roll the cutlet into a tight log and set aside, seam side down.

5. Tie the braciola. The simplest way is to use 2 or 3 short lengths of butcher's twine for each roll and tie them around the meat to hold it together. If you're a master of more professional ways of tying—like a real butcher's tie—go for it. But the braciola doesn't (or shouldn't) get roughed up too much during the cooking process, so it doesn't need to be in a straitjacket or anything. It's really as easy as . . .

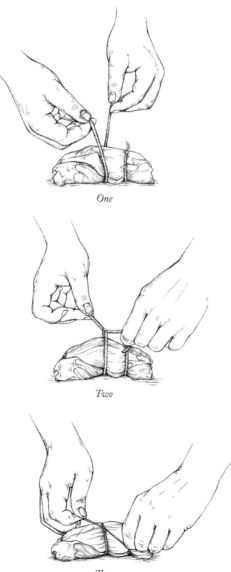

One

Two

Three

Finished Braciola Using This Tying Method

6. Bring the tomato sauce to a steady, gentle simmer in a large pot.

7. Nestle the braciola into the pot of tomato sauce. Simmer for 3 hours, or until tender; you should be able to easily pull away a strand or two of meat with the tug of a fork.

8. To serve, remove the braciola from the sauce and snip off the twine. Arrange, whole or sliced, on a platter with a generous blanket of sauce. Transfer the remaining sauce to a serving bowl. Serve hot or at room temperature. Garnish with grated Pecorino Romano and serve. Use leftover tomato sauce from the braciola in any recipe in this book that calls for tomato sauce.

VARIATION: HOME-STYLE BRACIOLA—*Our grandmas browned their braciola before they put it into the sauce to simmer. We don't. It's an effort that we feel really doesn't pay dividends. But if you want to do it grandma-style, here it is:*

After you've tied the braciola, put ¼ cup olive oil and ¼ cup grapeseed oil in a wide skillet over medium-high heat. When the oil is hot but not smoking, add the braciola and sear, rotating them every minute or so, until lightly and evenly browned; work in batches so as not to crowd the pan. Transfer the seared braciola to the large pot with the sauce. Make sure to allow enough time to sear all the rolls, get them into the sauce, and then get to church on time.

SAUSAGE WITH PEPPERS & ONIONS

Frankies is an Italian-American restaurant. We have to serve some kind of sausage and peppers. Our version is like a loose, barely integrated ragu, with all the elements cooked separately. Over grilled bread, it's a real layup. (Try it that way during the summer.) We put it over our Semolina Polenta (recipe follows) to give it a whiff of refinement.

The key, we think, is finding real Italian sausage. Real Italian sausage is fermented. It's not just chopped meat and seasonings stuffed into a length of intestine and twisted off into sausage shapes. That's bratwurst and a million other fresh sausages. For real Italian sausage, the meat is chopped and seasoned. Then a culture is added to the meat, and it is allowed to ferment briefly, which adds a whole layer of flavor—that funky, old-world tang that makes it so delicious. It's worth asking around at shops that carry Italian ingredients if they ferment their sausages (or if the salumi connection that supplies them does). If they don't know, the answer is probably no, though that wouldn't stop us from cooking up the sausages just like this.

Serves 6 to 8

4 bell peppers— 2 red and 2 yellow

1 large yellow onion

1 tablespoon grapeseed oil

Fine sea salt

2 pounds sweet Italian pork sausage, casings removed

2 cups Tomato Sauce (page xx) or one 28-ounce can San Marzano tomatoes

1. Roast the peppers: If you have a gas stove, turn the burners on high and lay a pepper on each. Roast, using tongs to turn the peppers every couple of minutes, until the skins are thoroughly blackened and blistered, about 7 minutes. If you don't have a gas range, you can roast the peppers over a hot fire on an outdoor grill, or gloss them with a little oil and roast them under the broiler, turning frequently, for about 15 minutes. Once the peppers are roasted, put them in a small mixing bowl, cover it with plastic wrap, and let them steam in the bowl.

2. When the peppers are cool enough to handle, core and seed them and scrape away as much of the blackened skin as possible. Slice the roasted peppers into ½-inch-wide strips and reserve.

3. Cut the onion in half through the root end, then cut the onion halves into ¼-inch-wide strips with the grain, meaning from the root end to the top. (Onions cut across the grain will melt into the sauce; onions cut with the grain will keep their shape.)

4. Heat the grapeseed oil in a wide sauté pan over medium-high heat. When the oil is hot, add the onion and a pinch of salt and cook, stirring occasionally, until the onion softens and starts to take on a golden color. Using a slotted spoon remove the onion from the pan and reserve. Without wiping out the pan or turning down the heat, add the sausage meat and sauté, jabbing at it with a wooden spoon to break up the clumps of meat, for 10 to 12 minutes, until browned but not dried out.

5. Add the tomato sauce (or the canned tomatoes, crushing them in your hands one by one as you add them to the pan) and scrape the bottom of the pan with the spoon to loosen any browned bits. Simmer for 15 to 30 minutes—however long you've got. Add the peppers and onions, stir together, and simmer for a few more minutes, until warmed through.

6. Serve the sausage and peppers hot, over the polenta, or with thick slices of good grilled or toasted bread.

Semolina Polenta (recipe follows) or grilled or toasted bread

SEMOLINA POLENTA

3½ cups Cheese
Broth (page 14)
or water

½ cup coarse-
ground semolina

2 tablespoons
unsalted butter

¼ cup grated
Pecorino Romano

2 tablespoons
pine nuts, plus a
handful of nuts
for garnish

Fine sea salt and
freshly ground
white pepper

Polenta is usually made with cornmeal. We make ours with semolina—coarse-ground hard wheat, the same thing that good dried pasta is made out of. It's silky smooth and way better than that cornmeal mush.

1. Bring the cheese broth to a boil in a medium saucepan over high heat. When it boils, add the semolina in a steady thin stream, stirring or whisking constantly. Stir or whisk for the first minute, then adjust the heat so the semolina simmers gently but steadily. Cook, stirring occasionally, for 45 minutes, or until the polenta is creamy and soft.

2. Stir in the butter, cheese, and pine nuts, add a pinch of salt and a few twists of white pepper, and taste to see if it needs any more anything. If serving the polenta as a side dish on its own, garnish it with pine nuts before serving.

EGGPLANT MARINARA

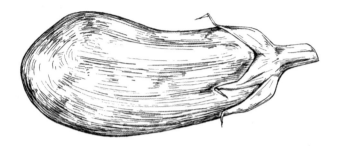

There are always these guys—big guys, Italian guys, the trash and construction-trade type guys—at the restaurant. Generally, they get it. But there are a few things that trip them up. This preparation is one of them. There's always something wrong with it. The eggplant isn't fried. The eggplant isn't breaded. Something about the cheese. And if they knew about the white pepper, it's hard to imagine what they'd think. So, no: this isn't anybody's grandma's eggplant Parmesan. We're not actually sorry about that.

At the restaurant we use it as a sandwich filling and serve it hot in a baking dish like a noodleless lasagna at parties out in the backyard. The best way to eat it is to sneak down into the kitchen after the cooks have made a batch, wait for a tray of it to cool to room temperature—a couple of hours out of the oven, just when the heat's gone but it hasn't yet met the cold of the fridge—and then attack it, sneaking away with a plateful to eat standing up somewhere.

With bread and a salad, this makes a perfect vegetarian main course for a group. Or, if you bake it on a Sunday afternoon, you can feed yourself from a tray of it for a couple of days.

> ***THE WAY WE USED TO DO IT**—We used to use twice as much mozzarella to make this. We'd lay it in the pan between each layer of eggplant. We've moved away from that method because the cheese takes on a strange though not unlikable rubberiness, and we don't like the way eating long-cooked cheese makes us feel. But, hey, if that's what you're into, it's cool. We were there once, too.*

Serves 4 to 6

**3 large eggplants
(a little more than
3 pounds total),
peeled in vertical
strips with a
vegetable peeler,
leaving alternating
strips of skin, and
sliced into ½-inch-
thick disks**

¼ cup olive oil

**Fine sea salt and
freshly ground
white pepper**

**About 3 cups
Tomato Sauce
(page xx)**

**3 cups grated
Pecorino Romano**

**½ ball fresh
mozzarella
(about 8 ounces),
cut into ¼-inch-
thick slices
(or, if you're feeling
fancy, 1 ball of
mozzarella di
bufala, sliced the
same way)**

1. Heat the oven to 350°F. Toss the sliced egg-plant with the olive oil, salt, and white pepper to taste in a large mixing bowl, making sure that the eggplant is evenly dressed. Arrange the eggplant slices in a single layer on two baking sheets.

2. Pop the eggplant into the oven and bake for 20 to 25 minutes, flipping it once midway, until it's lightly mottled in parts and deeply browned in others and beginning to—but not quite yet—shrink away from the skin. Remove from the oven (leaving the oven on).

3. Coat the bottom of a medium roasting pan (or other casserole or ovenproof vessel appropri-ate for a lasagna-type preparation) with a thin slick of tomato sauce. Nestle a single layer of eggplant slices into the sauce, sprinkle with salt and pepper, and give the eggplant a good coat-ing of Pecorino. Repeat until all the ingredients are used—sauce, eggplant, Pecorino—finishing with a layer of cheese. Cover the pan with foil and bake for 3½ hours.

4. Serve eggplant marinara hot, cold, or in between. Arrange a layer of the mozzarella slices over the top of the dish just before you serve it.

QUICK EGGPLANT FIX

If you don't have 4 hours to bake this thing and you don't have any tomato sauce ready, you can pull off a good approximation in about 2 hours start to finish.

Heat the oven to 350°F. Sprinkle the eggplant slices with salt—enough to coat them—and let sit for 15 to 30 minutes.

While the eggplant is sitting, start your sauce: combine 4 cloves of garlic and ½ cup of olive oil in a saucepan over low heat. Cook for about 10 minutes, stirring or swirling the pan occasionally, until the garlic is golden and fragrant. Keep the heat low. If the garlic starts to smell acrid or sharp or appears to be browning, pull the pan off the burner and reduce the heat.

While the garlic is getting golden, open a 28-ounce can of San Marzano tomatoes, pour them into a bowl, and crush them with your hands. After the garlic's been going for 10 minutes, dump in the tomatoes and add a tiny pinch of red pepper flakes and maybe a teaspoon of salt. Turn the heat to medium so the sauce simmers, but not too aggressively. Cook, stirring from time to time, while you do the eggplant.

Now the eggplant: Brush off any excess salt, but don't fret over it. Toss the eggplant slices with ½ cup olive oil and a few turns of white pepper. Arrange on a baking sheet and bake as directed in the recipe.

Okay, the eggplant is baked and the sauce has had as much time as you have for it to cook. Assemble the dish as directed in the recipe and bake it for as long as possible. After an hour or so, you should be good.

SWEET-AND-SOUR BAKED EGGPLANT WITH MINT & RICOTTA SALATA

We picked up this preparation in Sicily, where they're totally attuned to the affinity that eggplant has for sugar. This is a good way to vary the routine when you burn out on the Eggplant Marinara.

*Serves 6 as
an appetizer*

¼ cup water

¼ cup sugar

¼ cup wine vinegar

One 28-ounce
can San Marzano
tomatoes, crushed
by hand

2 garlic cloves,
thinly sliced

½ cup extra virgin
olive oil

Fine sea salt and
freshly ground
white pepper

2 large eggplants
(about 1¼ pounds
each), sliced into
¾-inch-thick disks

½ cup shredded
ricotta salata

¼ cup chopped
mint

1. Combine the water and sugar in a small sauce-pan and stir over high heat until the sugar dissolves. Cook without stirring until a light amber caramel forms. Off the heat, add the vinegar; be careful—it will bubble furiously. Cook over very low heat just until the caramel dissolves again, about 1 minute.

2. Add the crushed tomatoes, garlic, and ¼ cup of oil to the caramel. Season with salt and white pepper. Simmer over moderately low heat until sauce is thickened, about 30 minutes.

3. Meanwhile, preheat the oven to 400°F. Brush a large baking sheet with 2 tablespoons of oil. Arrange the eggplant on the sheet, brush with the remaining 2 tablespoons oil, and season with salt and pepper. Roast the eggplant 10 minutes, then flip and roast for 10 minutes longer, or until tender and lightly golden. Remove from the oven (leaving the oven on).

4. Arrange the eggplant slices in slightly over-lapping rows in an 8-by-11-inch baking dish. Spoon two-thirds of the tomato sauce on top and bake for 20 minutes, or until bubbling and browned around the edges.

5. Sprinkle with cheese and mint and serve, pass-ing the remaining sauce on the side.

BRAISED SHORT RIBS

We served this for the first time as a New Year's Eve special. It got such a good response that we tried it out on the regular menu. Now it's a winter staple, one of those dishes that's a perfect rebuttal to gray-sky, leafless winter days.

Serves 4

4 pounds short ribs (4 big ribs, or 8 pieces if they've been cut crosswise)

Fine sea salt and freshly ground white pepper

2 tablespoons grapeseed or olive oil, plus a splash more later

1 yellow onion, quartered

1 carrot, unpeeled, cut into 1-inch chunks

1 or 2 stalks celery, cut into 1-inch chunks

1 small fennel bulb (or ½ large bulb), cut into 1-inch pieces

1 large sprig rosemary

(ingredients continued on next page)

1. Heat the oven to 400°F. Season the ribs generously with salt and white pepper. Put them on a baking sheet, pop it into the oven, and roast until the ribs have begun to brown and shrink away from the bones, about 45 minutes. Remove the meat to a platter to rest. Turn the oven down to 300°F.

2. While the beef is browning, heat the oil in your widest skillet or sauté pan over high heat for 1 minute, then add the onion, carrot, celery, and fennel and turn the heat down to medium-high. Add a large pinch of salt and sauté until the mass of vegetables has shrunken and begun to take on a golden caramel color, browning in spots, about 20 minutes. Remove from the heat.

3. Put the roasted ribs in a 6- or 8-quart heavy-bottomed ovenproof pot (a Dutch oven works great). Add the cooked vegetables, rosemary, red wine, and enough veal stock to almost but not quite cover the meat. Cover the pot and pop it into the oven. Braise for 2 to 2½ hours, at which point the bones should slide easily out of the meat.

4. Remove the meat from the pot, then strain the cooking liquid into a container (or two), pressing slightly hard on the vegetables in the strainer to wring out any flavor left in them.

1 cup dry red wine

4 cups Veal Stock (page 145) or water

Serving vegetables: 4 cups total, preferably a mix of peeled white baby turnips, peeled carrots cut on the bias into 1-inch chunks, and peeled pearl onions

Discard the vegetables. Cover the broth, cool to room temperature, and put in the fridge. (The meat and the broth can be held in the refrigerator for up to 2 days.)

5. When ready to serve, coat the serving vegetables with a film of olive oil and season with salt and white pepper, as you would in making any of the roasted vegetable antipasti on pages 34–45. Cook them for 20 minutes.

6. While the vegetables are roasting, remove the hardened cap of tallow-colored fat from the top of the braising liquid, discard it, and then put the liquid in a wide, deep pan and warm it over medium heat. Taste it. If it's thin, boil it down to concentrate it. Does it need salt? Add it. Perfect? Pour yourself a glass of wine and get back to work.

7. Trim the short ribs of any obvious gristle and cut them into individual portions.

8. Add the roasted vegetables to the warmed braising liquid and simmer for 10 minutes. Then add the meat. (You can hold the braise for up to a couple of hours at a very low temperature or serve as soon as the meat is warmed through.)

9. Serve the ribs in shallow bowls, with a mix of vegetables and some of the braising liquid.

BRAISED PORK SHANK WITH GIGANTE BEANS & ROSEMARY

After a couple of years of rocking the braciola, meatballs, and short ribs, we were looking for something new for the wintertime. It had to be a cheap cut and a dish where most of the work could be finished ahead of time. Pork shanks made their way to the front of the list immediately. We'd had them very simply braised at Ardigna, a family restaurant in the mountains of western Sicily, as part of a spread that included warm beans and creamy soft polenta. The beans became part of the Spuntino preparation; our recipe for Semolina Polenta, should you want to invite it to the party, is on page 136.

1. Heat the oven to 300°F. In a wide, deep pan (a 4-quart sautoir or a Dutch oven), heat the oil over medium-high heat. While the oil is heating, generously season the shanks with salt and white pepper. Add them to the pan, fleshier-side down, and brown for 8 to 10 minutes, until the meat is a deep golden brown and releases from the pan easily.

2. Remove the meat from the pan, transfer it to a plate, and hold it there. Add the onion, carrot, celery, and fennel to the pan. Add a large pinch of salt, stir the vegetables to mix it in, and sweat them for 8 to 10 minutes, stirring occasionally, until they've softened and shrunk.

3. Return the shanks to the pan. Add the garlic, bay leaves, and two sprigs of rosemary. Add the veal stock (or water) and supplemental water as needed to fully submerge the meat. Cover with a lid or (more carefully) with a couple of sheets of foil, and put the pan in the oven.

Serves 4

1 tablespoon grapeseed oil

4 pork shanks, about 4 pounds

Fine sea salt

Freshly ground white pepper

1 large yellow onion, quartered

1 large carrot, chopped

1 stalk celery, chopped

1 cup roughly chopped fennel

1 head garlic, cut in half crosswise

(ingredients continued on next page)

2 bay leaves

2 sprigs fresh rosemary, plus 4 additional sprigs for serving

4 cups Veal Stock (recipe follows) or water

Serving vegetables: 4 cups total, preferably a mix of peeled white baby turnips, peeled carrots cut on the bias into 1-inch chunks, and peeled pearl onions

2 tablespoons butter

Gigante Beans, (recipe follows), warm

4. Braise the meat for 3 to 3½ hours. It should give easily to a tug from a fork. Remove the pan to the stove top (or a trivet on a counter) and let the shanks come to room temperature in the broth.

5. Once the pan is cool, remove the shanks from the broth and reserve them. (The shanks can be wrapped in plastic and stored in the refrigerator for up to 2 days at this point.) Strain the vegetables from the broth (wrenching as much liquid as possible out of them before discarding them) and return the broth to the stove. Boil it over high heat until it has been reduced to half its original volume. The broth can be cooled to room temperature and stored in the refrigerator alongside the shanks at this point; otherwise, proceed.

6. Bring the broth to a simmer, taste it, and season with salt as needed. Add the serving vegetables and the additional rosemary to the pan and simmer for 12 to 15 minutes, until the vegetables are tender enough that they offer almost no resistance to the tip of a thin-bladed knife. Add the shanks to the pan and warm them through, about 15 minutes. Stir in the butter once the shanks are warm.

7. Ladle out a generous half cup or so of beans into each of four shallow bowls. Divide the shanks and simmered vegetables among the serving bowls, add ¼ cup of the broth to each, and serve.

GIGANTE BEANS

Gigante beans are an oversized variety most commonly seen in Greek cuisine. They're easy to find in specialty stores here in New York. If you can't track them down, feel free to swap in dried cannellini beans.

1. Soak the beans in water to cover for at least 6 hours and as long as overnight.

2. Drain the beans and put them in a pot. Add water to cover, the herbs, and one large pinch of salt. Bring to a boil over high heat. Reduce the heat to low and simmer for two hours, until tender, replenishing water as necessary.

3. Drain the beans and discard the herbs. Season the beans with an additional pinch of salt.

Makes about 2 cups

Heaping ½ cup dried gigante beans

A few sprigs rosemary

A few sprigs thyme

Fine sea salt

VEAL STOCK

The particular combination of veal bones is not important. We usually get a mix of leg bones and knuckles, but sometimes you get lucky and end up with shanks—osso buco—and then you get some meat off them.

The only tweak we make on this otherwise straight-ahead classic is swapping celery root for celery, because we always have it on hand for our Fennel, Celery Root, Parsley & Red Onion Salad (page 84). You can use either, though the root adds an appealing sweetness.

Makes at least 2 quarts

5 to 6 pounds veal bones

3 small or 2 medium onions, coarsely chopped

(ingredients continued on next page)

1 large or
2 medium carrots,
peeled and coarsely
chopped

1 cup roughly
chopped celery
root

A leek, chopped,
if you've got one
around

1 bay leaf

A few sprigs each
rosemary and
thyme

A bunch's worth of
parsley stems

1. Heat the oven to 400°F. Arrange the veal bones on a rimmed baking sheet with a bit of space between them. Roast them for 30 to 45 minutes, until they've started to brown and they smell good and roasted.

2. Transfer the bones to a large stockpot. Cover with water and bring to a boil over high heat. As it comes to a boil and in the few minutes after, skim the scummy foam the bones throw off.

3. When it does boil, reduce the heat to low, so the liquid lazily simmers and burbles, add your vegetables and herbs, and simmer uncovered for 4 hours.

4. When the stock's done its simmering, strain it, discarding the vegetables and bones. You can use the stock straightaway, refrigerate it for up to five days, or freeze it. (It's best used within a couple of months.) If you want, reduce it so it takes up less space in the fridge or freezer. (Just remember to dilute it when you use it.)

BIG MEAT

Big cuts of meat—like an imposing six-rib pork roast or a hulking five-pound rib eye—are some of our favorite things to cook at Frankies. Why? We could tell you about how we grew up in big families who got together for big meals and that cuts like these were always a treat. We could tell you that we like them because they're regal, impressive cuts, protein perfection on the plate that everybody digs on.

But the real reason to cook cuts like these is that they couldn't be easier to get right. Try to broil or grill or pan-sear six rib-eye steaks for your friends and have them all out on the table, perfectly cooked and hot at the same time. Can you do it? Sure, with a little practice. But you'll be spent, the stove or grill will be a mess, and the results won't win you any more points than either of the following two recipes.

At the restaurant we cook the rib eye during the summer and serve it cold with sliced tomatoes and red onions, everything doused with olive oil. The pig takes over when the weather turns. A thick slice of the roasted rack, a puddle of warm Semolina Polenta (page 136) and a side of broccoli rabe (pinched from the antipasto platters) anchors the winter menu. At home, accompany either of them as you see fit. If you have the space, serve these big cuts family-style, with starches and vegetables passed on separate platters.

A couple of pointers:

Flavor the meat early, with the herbs and garlic, but save the salt for just before you cook it.

Roast it slow and low. After an initial blast of heat to help get the meat browning, we turn it down low. Treat the meat nicely and it'll repay the favor.

Let it rest, rest, rest, and then rest some more. Meat is muscle, and it contracts when it cooks. Let it relax; relaxed meat is better to eat. And always taste it before serving. We usually find that a sprinkle of salt over each portion is a good idea.

SLOW-ROASTED RIB EYE, SLICED COLD

We slow roast the rib eye, let it rest, and then chill it. And then a very special thing happens: it magically becomes the best roast beef ever. Not your deli-variety roast beef, but a thoroughbred version of it.

Serve the beef with some kind of salad, like the Tomato, Avocado & Red Onion Salad on page 81 or a few tomatoes and red onions simply sliced and seasoned with olive oil, salt, and black pepper.

Serves 6 to 9, though you wouldn't want to end up without leftovers

1 sprig rosemary, leaves stripped and finely chopped

1 tablespoon finely chopped thyme leaves

2 tablespoons finely chopped flat-leaf parsley

4 cloves garlic, finely chopped

2 tablespoons olive oil

One 2½- to 3-pound boneless rib-eye roast

1 tablespoon fine sea salt

Freshly ground white pepper

1. Combine the herbs, garlic, and olive oil in a small bowl. Smear this mixture all over the beef. Put the beef in a baking dish, cover, and allow to season in the refrigerator for as long as 24 hours.

2. Heat the oven to 375°F. Put the beef in a roasting pan or on a rimmed baking sheet (it shouldn't render too much fat during cooking) and rub it all over with the salt and white pepper to taste.

3. Pop the beef into the oven. After 15 minutes, turn the heat down to 325°F. Roast for 45 minutes more, or until a thermometer inserted into the thickest part of the rib eye reads 118°F. Remove the beef from the pan and let it rest, uncovered, for at least 45 minutes.

4. Wrap the beef in plastic, put it in the fridge, and hold it for up to a couple of days before serving.

5. Cut the beef into ½-inch-thick slices and serve.

Roast Center-Cut Pork Chops

This is a menu stalwart during the winter months at the restaurant. If you want to make it even further in advance than this recipe calls for, allow it to rest as directed in Step 4, then wrap it tightly in plastic and refrigerate for up to 2 days. Cut the rack into chops and warm them through in butter in a sauté pan over medium heat.

Serves 6

1 sprig rosemary, leaves stripped and finely chopped

2 tablespoons finely chopped thyme leaves

2 tablespoons finely chopped flat-leaf parsley

6 cloves garlic, finely chopped

¼ cup olive oil

One 6-bone center-cut rack of pork (about 6 pounds), chine bone removed by the butcher

2 tablespoons fine sea salt

Freshly ground white pepper

For serving:

Semolina Polenta (page 136)

1 double recipe Broccoli Rabe (page 38)

1. Combine the herbs, garlic, and olive oil in a small bowl. Smear this mixture all over the pork, then put the pork in a baking dish, cover, and allow it to sit, refrigerated, for at least 6 hours and up to 24.

2. Heat the oven to 400°F. Put the rack of pork in a roasting pan or on a baking sheet (it shouldn't render too much fat during cooking) and season with salt and white pepper to taste.

3. Pop the pork into the oven. After 20 minutes, turn the heat down to 325°F. Roast for about 1 hour and 20 minutes more, until the pork is just past rare—still a shade pink in the center of the roast. An instant-read thermometer should read 135° to 140°F. Remove the pork from the oven and allow to rest, uncovered, for 30 minutes.

4. Slice the pork into individual chops and serve with Semolina Polenta and Broccoli Rabe.

CHAPTER 7

SUNDAY SAUCE

Sunday sauce—the meal, the menu, the way of life—is the source and the summation of Frankies Spuntino.

We were both raised in Italian-American families that did the whole get-everybody-together thing on Sundays. It was almost always at one of our grandmothers' houses in the just-after-church hours. (Sometimes when we were teenagers, we'd slink over as late as 2 or 3 P.M., but the spread would be pretty picked over by then.)

Our grandmothers and mothers made the Sunday sauce happen. The work started on Saturday, with trips to the butcher, the deli, and the supermarket to buy the fresh and cured meats, cheeses, and canned tomatoes, and whatever vegetables were needed. On Sunday morning, earlier than early, they'd be in the kitchen squeezing tomatoes and starting the sauce on its long, slow simmer, the smell of tomatoes rising with the sun before they were out the door and off to six o'clock mass.

After mass, coffee goes on, and the cooking gets more serious. These early quiet hours are a good time to get fresh pasta made, dusted with flour, and perched precariously on a cookie sheet in the fridge. As the morning matures, the daughters (our moms and aunts) complete their obligations to the church and head over and into the kitchen. One of them picks up the cannoli and sfogliatelle and sesame bread from the bakery on the way over.

Meatballs are shaped as the kids are assessed. (There's always somebody to fret over.) At some point, Grandma slips the braciola (which she bought pre-tied at the butcher's or took care of the night before) into the sauce. The kitchen starts to fill with that hunger-inducing humidity, the tomato and pork simmering away in the pot. The oven door squeaks open, and the sharp sizzle announces that this is a Sunday when Grandma is roasting a chicken, too.

The nieces start to set the table. The dads and uncles, who begin to make peckish incursions into the kitchen sanctuary, are tasked with laying out the capicola or prosciutto, and they inevitably eat half of it in the process. Olives and artichokes and roasted peppers, purchased at the deli, are put in bowls and placed on the table. If nobody made fresh pasta, a couple of boxes of rigatoni are boiled and tossed with the tomato sauce in which the meatballs and braciola, and sometimes pork ribs, have been cooking. The sauce is red and smooth, glossy with fat and flecked with stray meat or cheese or parsley stems.

Out comes the gigantic salad bowl, and heaps of bitter greens or a few heads of chopped iceberg lettuce are dressed with glugs of olive oil and red wine vinegar. Bottles of red wine, basement cold, are set on the sideboard, open for anybody to drink.

And now, a couple of huge serving trays emerge from the kitchen carrying the Sunday sauce; bowls of meatballs and braciola are mainstays. If sausage ("it was on special at the store") or lamb neck (for Grandpa) makes an appearance, it's been simmered in its own pot of tomato sauce to quarantine the assertive flavors.

Eventually the table is so full that sitting around it is impractical. The uncles and dads splinter off to the living room to eat off plates on their laps and talk about cars. Grandma and a couple of her daughters eat in the kitchen, and the kids run about and eat wherever.

After a couple of hours, mountains of food have been consumed, and the Tupperware comes out to house the leftovers that are sent home with our parents. Our grandmas know what a growing boy's appetite is like.

CASTRONOVO ON THE SUNDAY SAUCE

My maternal grandma passed away when I was pretty young, and from then on in it was all about Sundays at my great-grandma DiLeo's. We called her Grandma Brooklyn, which helped sort her out from my paternal grandmother in the Bronx. She lived in a railroad flat in Williamsburg, Brooklyn.

Now I know how Italians talk about their grandma's food and say it was the best. For the record, my grandma's cooking really *was* the best. She was a chef in Italy before she came to America and became a housewife. She worked for a don or a duke, a member of one of the richest families in Naples.

Sundays were for eating and hanging out with the family—cousins, uncles, aunts, grandparents, great-grandparents. Even when I was a teenager and wanted to be a punk and went to matinée shows at CBGB, I'd still stop and eat at my grandma's house before the rest of the day went down. I liked to get there either before 9:30 in the morning (because she'd slip me a fiver as a bonus for going to 10 o'clock mass with her) or after 11:30 A.M. if I wasn't in the mood to sit through a sermon.

The women stayed in the kitchen helping with the food and the men hung out in the living room. By noon, or a little after, the food was on the table: the huge pot of sauce with the meat; the braciola, lamb necks, pork ribs, and meatballs. There was also pasta or lasagna, a salad or two, and usually some kind of chicken. Afterward, there was a homemade dessert or a box of cannoli from the bakery. Then everybody would scavenge the leftovers: meatballs sent home in Tupperware, braciola dispatched for eating cold out of the fridge later that night. We'd all head home, and seven days later do it all over again.

FALCINELLI ON THE SUNDAY SAUCE

The generations of Falcinellis and Martuccis that came before mine canned the tomatoes they grew in their backyards and made wine in their basements. Back in my great-grandparents' and my grandparents' generations, if you didn't know how to make wine, you weren't drinking. If you didn't grow and can tomatoes, the winters would be especially harsh. My grandparents had all of those skills.

But by the time my parents came of age in the 1950s, and I was growing up in the 1970s, a lot of that knowledge had begun to die off. My parents and I keep traditions alive because they are part of our heritage—rituals to mark the passing of the seasons. They also happen to be fun. But it isn't live-or-die information: Today you can buy amazing Italian canned tomatoes for just pennies more than crappy American ones. We still like to can tomatoes at the end of the summer, because they make good Christmas gifts. We also make wine once a year in the fall, mainly for kicks, on the anniversary of the restaurant's opening day.

My family still gets together on Sunday afternoons just as it always has, and the food is the same as it ever was—the red-sauce parade of meatballs, short ribs, and braciola with rigatoni or gnocchi or fusilli. Growing up, I didn't see it as an amazing culinary tradition, but I did appreciate how good the eating was. My friends were eating gray pot roast, burnt biscuits, and army green peas while I was eating delicious meals drenched in pork-infused tomato sauce. And that was my main inspiration for opening the Spuntino: to create a place where every day feels like Sunday.

SUNDAY SAUCE ESSENTIALS

SNACKS

Refer to the antipasto chapter. You're going to the store the day before anyway. Stock up on salumi, cheeses, and olives for your family to graze on while you pull the meal together.

SALAD

Check out the options in the salad chapter. If you can't manage any of those, toss some greens with olive oil, lemon juice, and salt. There's got to be a salad.

PASTA

Again, there's a chapter's worth of good ideas between these covers. Making fresh gnocchi or cavatelli will earn you extra love and affection, though we've never heard anybody complain when Grandma boiled up a couple of boxes of rigatoni. If simplicity is the goal, dress the pasta with ladles of red from the saucepot or in melted butter and grated Parmesan.

THE SAUCE

It's a cauldron of crushed canned Italian tomatoes in which a variety of meats have been simmered. Meatballs and braciola are the don't-pass-go standbys in our repertory, but for a real Sunday sauce, you want both of these plus a third option, to add to the abundance. The two easiest choices are ribs and sausage.

Pork ribs are a cheap option that everybody will gobble down: Buy a rack or two, season them liberally with salt and white pepper, and cut them into 2- or 3-rib sections (or ask your butcher to do the prep). Roast in the oven at 350°F for 40 minutes, then simmer in some of the tomato sauce, in a separate pot, until tender, for 2 or more hours.

Italian sausage, sweet or hot, is great, but it's usually seasoned so strongly that it can overpower the tomato sauce. If you're going to do sausage, make your sauce, get your braciola cooked, and then, in the last 30 minutes, while the meatballs are cooking, scoop a quart or two of the tomato sauce into a smaller pot and simmer the sausage in that. You can brown the sausage in a skillet beforehand, but we don't think doing that really adds much to the finished product.

Beyond those two, well, Castronovo's grandfather loved it when his wife would braise him his own pot of lamb neck, and Falcinelli's Grandma Anne used to do short ribs for a special Sunday every now and again. We've done pork belly, pork skin, braciola with beef instead of pork, you name it. The moral of the story is that you can braise almost any meat in a pot of tomato sauce and it's gonna come out good. Just allow enough time for the meat to fully braise (tough cuts like neck and short ribs need up to 3 or 4 hours) and make sure to segregate stronger-flavored meats—like lamb, seasoned meats, or sausage—in their own pots so their flavor doesn't take over the whole show.

Consider doubling the tomato sauce recipe (26 cloves' worth of garlic). That stuff is red gold after you've simmered braciola and meatballs and whatever else you put into it, and it can be portioned out into quart containers and frozen for future use.

SUNDAY SAUCE: THE TIMELINE

SATURDAY
Check the cupboard, make a list, and go shopping.

Stop 1
The Grocery Store

GROCERY STORE

Vegetables/Fruit
    Several heads of garlic
    Flat-leaf parsley
    Baking potatoes, if you're making gnocchi
Pantry
    Olive oil
    Canned tomatoes
    Raisins
    Pine nuts
    Fine sea salt
    White peppercorns
    Red pepper flakes
    Flour
Dairy Section (or Cheese Shop)
    Eggs
    Pecorino Romano
    Provolone, for making braciola if you're doing that, and for snacking
    Ricotta, for cavatelli or for crostini
    Cheeses for antipasto

SATURDAY (cont.)

*When you're at the deli or the butcher shop make sure to get
a few different meats and cheeses and olives for the antipasto. Buy bread, or give someone else the job of picking it
up. That's how it always went down with our families.*

*Stop 2
The Butcher Shop*

BUTCHER SHOP

1. Cured meats to serve as antipasto
2. Ground beef for meatballs (90% lean)
3. ½ pound of ½-inch-thick boneless pork shoulder steaks
   if you have to make your own braciola (we usually buy
   ours from a trusted Italian butcher)
4. Optional additional meat such as sausage, pork ribs, or
   beef short ribs

*If you don't have a butcher who makes braciola that you like, we
advise rolling and tying the braciola (see pages 130–133) the day
before.*

Dessert's an important consideration. If you're going to make the Ricotta Cheesecake (page 169) or something equally impressive, make sure you have both the ingredients and the time to prepare it. Otherwise, plan a trip to the bakery or put somebody you're going to be feeding on pick-up-the-cannoli duty.

Stop 3
The Bakery

BAKERY

1. Fresh bread
2. Bread crumbs
3. Dessert
 (assuming you're not making it)

CAVEAT

We are not our grandmothers. Wish we had their stamina. But
without the piety to drag yourself out of bed before dawn, getting
a Sunday sauce meal on the table by the early afternoon can be
daunting. If you change "7 A.M." to noon, as we often do, you'll have
the feast on the table by 6 P.M.

*6 A.M. Go to mass. Bonus: the homilies are shorter, as are the lines for
communion. You get in and out and back to the kitchen faster.*

SUNDAY

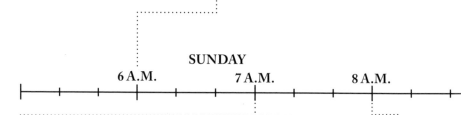

6 A.M.   7 A.M.   8 A.M.

*7 A.M. Turn the oven to 350°F. It begins with the tomato
sauce (see page xx): Start the garlic in the oil while you
crush the tomatoes. Give the sauce 30 to 45 minutes to
simmer and start to meld, and, if you're doing ribs, pop
them in the oven to brown.*

*8 A.M. Turn the tomato sauce down to a nice, steady, gentle temperature
and add the braciola. When the ribs have finished their 40 minutes of
oven time, add them to the pot. Mix and shape the meatballs (see page
124) and put them in the oven to bake once the ribs have slipped into
the tomato sauce hot tub.*

9 A.M. *Make fresh pasta (unless you're using rigatoni); if ease is important, do cavatelli (see pages 100).*

10 A.M. *If you're going to make some vegetable anti-pasti, now's the time. We'd strongly recommend two or more vegetables, selected from the antipasto section (page 34–45). The leftovers will be the reward.*

If you're making crostini to go with the meal, it's time to puree the parsley into pesto.

SUNDAY

9 A.M.   10 A.M.   11 A.M.

11 A.M. *Get your salad fixings ready: Clean the lettuces, make the vinaigrette, etc. Don't make or dress the salad at this point, but have everything ready to assemble, like you're a TV chef.*

Put out the cured meats and cheeses and olives. Skim the fat off the top of the tomato sauce. Show one of your guests how to assemble the crostini and then put them to work.

Noon. Take the braciola out, stack them up on a plate, and hold them at room temperature. (Castronovo's grandma used to cut the twine off them, making them easier to eat. We do that at the restaurant but skip it at home. Just make sure there are sharp knives on the table.)

If you made pork ribs, stack them up on another plate. Put the meatballs in the sauce to simmer for 30 minutes.

12:30 P.M. Ask family members or guests to set the table, etc.

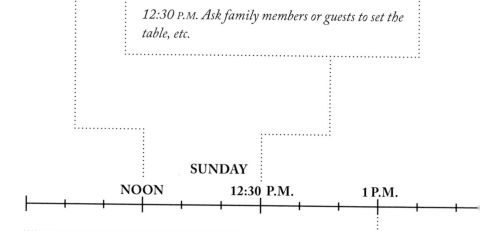

SUNDAY

NOON   12:30 P.M.   1 P.M.

1 P.M. Just before you're ready to eat, combine the braciola, meatballs, optional third meat, and a goodly amount of tomato sauce in a roasting pan. Put it in the oven or over a burner to warm through. Cook and sauce the pasta, and put it out on the table. Shepherd the leftover antipasto to the table. Slice some bread. Toss the salad. Make sure there's wine open; you'll need some.

Dig in. Eat and enjoy. Deny that it was any work when everybody asks if you're tired.

Do it every Sunday.

Do it forever.

MONDAY

THE NEXT DAY

There will be leftovers. If there are not, that's okay. You didn't make that bad a mistake, but in the future, adjust up. Leftovers are part of what makes the work worthwhile.

Meatball Marinara Sandwiches (page 58) are a solid option; we regularly took them to school for lunch on Mondays. Castronovo's kids love leftover braciola, sliced thin, turned into sandwiches. You can use some of that meat-infused tomato sauce to dress a batch of Potato Gnocchi (page 98) during the week. But the real prize, at least for us, is turning the leftovers into lasagna.

Our moms and grandmas made lasagna only when other stuff was around. After a nice Sunday sauce, the fridge would be full—six sausages nobody had room for on a plate next to a bowl with four meatballs and maybe some braciola.

On Monday or Tuesday, they'd go to the store and buy a container of ricotta and a box of noodles, spend an hour in the kitchen, and conjure a tray of lasagna. Lasagna is a dense, formidable food, perfect when you're a hungry kid looking to eat on the run: a wallop of calories in no time at all, so fast nobody even sees you eat it. A family can live off a lasagna for a day or two, and we often did. When we were kids, both of us loved it cold as a snack out of the fridge and we still do.

LEFTOVERS LASAGNA

One 8-by-10-inch pan's worth

Fine sea salt

2 pounds lasagna noodles

¼ cup olive oil

1 large egg, beaten

3 cups ricotta

1 pound (4 to 6) sweet Italian sausages (or bake the sausages at 350°F for 30 minutes for this purpose), roughly chopped

6 leftover meatballs, crumbled

8 cups warm Tomato Sauce (page xx), possibly more for serving

Freshly ground black pepper

2 cups grated Pecorino Romano

1 pound mozzarella, cut into ¼-inch-thick slices

1. Heat the oven to 350°F. Bring a large pot of water to a boil and salt it well. Boil the lasagna noodles according to the package directions minus 90 seconds. Drain the noodles and lay them out on a baking sheet. Coat them with 2 tablespoons of the olive oil and allow them to cool.

2. Stir the egg into the ricotta. Mix the sausage and meatballs together.

3. Build it! From the bottom up: tomato sauce, black pepper, lasagna noodles, heaping table-spoon-sized lumps of meat with an inch or so between them, plops of ricotta where there are open spaces, a generous hit of grated cheese, and a blanket of mozzarella over all of that, more tomato sauce. Repeat until the pan is full. Finish with a noodle layer dressed with grated cheese and the remaining 2 tablespoons olive oil.

4. Cook it: Cover the pan with foil and bake for 20 minutes. Uncover and bake for another 10 minutes.

CHAPTER 8

DESSERTS

When we were growing up, there was always something around to eat for dessert.

At the Falcinellis, there was usually something from the supermarket during the week, like a box of Entenmann's doughnuts or Stella d'Oro cookies (which inspired the Chocolate Tart on page 172). On the weekend, his mom would line up for cookies and cannoli at one of the Italian pastry shops in the neighborhood or pick up a cake at Victor's (always Victor's) if there was a birthday on the horizon. Holidays and Sundays were when Mom would bust out the Ricotta Cheesecake (page 169).

Same thing at Castronovo's house: the handcrafted desserts were for Christmas and special occasions. His grandma even used to make a croquembouche-like tower of honey-glazed fritters for Easter. But most of the time it was fresh fruit, dried fruit, and always a huge bowl of walnuts in the shell to be cracked and eaten to accompany coffee after dinner.

All this backstory is a way of saying: Remember to have something sweet on hand to end the meal, but don't double over backward trying to make a big production of dessert. If you're pressed for time, the prunes recipe on page 168 can be made in advance, warmed, and served over a smushed scoop of mascarpone. Or make the Hazelnut Panna Cotta (page 176) first and then get to making the savory part of dinner. By the time everyone is done eating, lingering, and washing up, dessert will be ready.

Vanilla Bean Crème Brûlée

Frank Castronovo on crème brûlée (and a trip to France): When I went to France in my early twenties, I took only my bike, my knives, letters of recommendation, and a couple of changes of clothes. I started in Paris and biked south, cycling from one Michelin-starred restaurant to the next, in search of a job. I was rejected at every turn, but there are worse fates than biking through France. One afternoon, mostly on a lark, I started pedaling in the direction of Lyon with the goal of checking out the flagship restaurant belonging to one of the finest chefs of the twentieth century, the great Paul Bocuse. (Ever seen the kids' movie *Ratatouille*? The chef in the film is based on Bocuse.)

On the road, a guy in a sporty little car slowed down and checked out my bike and then sped off. He looked like a cook to me. When I got to the restaurant, I hid my bike in the bushes and switched from my bike gear into a suit and wingtips. I patted down my hair and knocked on the kitchen door. The guy who answered the door looked me over and asked, "Didn't I just see you on a bike?" He and another cook came over and checked out my cycling setup—I had everything in the world that was mine on it, neatly folded and compartmentalized. You would never have guessed a knife roll-up and a suit were in there.

I spent three-and-a-half amazing months interning in the kitchen at Bocuse after that. When my cash ran out and it was time to return to New York, the restaurant's chef de cuisine, Jean Fleury, called a chef named David Bouley in New York and asked him to hire me. When Paul Bocuse asks, the answer is always yes.

I learned a lot in my short time at Bocuse, but the one recipe that I've served at every restaurant I've worked at ever since—just because it's so popular—is the crème brûlée I learned to make there. There's nothing difficult about the recipe, but it does require some specialized equipment: You need ramekins (four-inch-long fluted ovals, less than an inch deep, so the ratio of crisp burnt sugar to supple custard is just right) and a kitchen blowtorch, which you can find at any hardware store. And with this particular recipe's perfect proportion of cream to milk, and a fresh vanilla bean for flavor, it's a dessert that's guaranteed to please.

1. Heat the oven to 300°F. Whisk the egg yolks together in a large bowl.

2. Combine the cream, milk, and sugar in a medium saucepan. Scrape the seeds from the vanilla bean and add the seeds and bean to the saucepan. Heat over medium-low heat until the mixture is warm to the touch. Add a ladleful of the warm mixture to the yolks, whisking constantly, then add the rest of the cream, whisking until the mixture is homogenous and smooth.

3. Set 8 crème brûlée ramekins in a large roasting pan. Ladle the cream mixture into the ramekins. To make a water bath, add hot water to the pan to come halfway up the sides of the ramekins. Cover the baking sheet with aluminum foil.

4. Carefully transfer the pan to the oven and cook the custards for 45 minutes, or until they are set but still jiggle softly when shaken. Put the ramekins in the fridge to chill. They'll be ready in a couple of hours and will keep for a couple of days. (If you're storing them for more than a few hours, or if your fridge is crammed with cheeses and meats and vegetables that you don't want the crème brûlée to taste like, wrap each ramekin in plastic wrap.)

5. To serve, sprinkle the top of each custard with enough raw sugar to cover it evenly. Crank up the propane torch. Working quickly, burn the sugar until it's dark and crisp. Serve while the sugar topping is still a little warm and the custard is still cold.

Serves 8

8 large egg yolks

2⅔ cups heavy cream

1⅓ cups whole milk

¾ cup granulated sugar

1 vanilla bean, split

½ to ¾ cup raw sugar (turbinado or Demerara)

RED WINE PRUNES
WITH MASCARPONE

This dish was inspired by a dessert of stewed dates made by a chef named Mark Ladner—Mario Batali's right-hand man—and filtered through the lens of Falcinelli's formative years in the southwest of France, where prunes are king. The result combines the heady aroma of cinnamon and hot wine; the sweet, meaty plumpness of braised prunes; and the clean, rich density of mascarpone.

Serves 6

**1 pound
(2 generous cups)
pitted prunes**

1¼ cups sugar

1 cinnamon stick

**2½ cups red wine
(a bottle, minus a
glass for the cook)**

**Two 8-ounce
containers
mascarpone cheese**

1. Combine the prunes, sugar, cinnamon, and wine in a small pot and bring to a boil over medium-high heat. Reduce the heat to medium low, so the liquid simmers very gently, and stew for 45 minutes, until the wine is syrupy and redolent of cinnamon. Remove the pot from the heat and discard the cinnamon stick. Let the prunes stand for at least 15 minutes before serving. This allows them to cool slightly (they should be warm to lukewarm when served) and absorb as much of the wine syrup as possible. The prunes can be prepared ahead of time. Once cooled, they will keep in their cooking liquid, in a covered container in the refrigerator, for up to a week. Gently rewarm them over low heat before serving.

2. Spread a mound of mascarpone—2½ to 3 tablespoons' worth—into a circular smear on each serving plate. Nestle 6 prunes in the center of each portion of mascarpone, then drizzle the prunes with a spoonful of the syrup and serve.

RICOTTA CHEESECAKE

Our chocolate is an adaptation of a recipe from Falcinelli's mom, Marie, who made it with a graham cracker crust instead of the pastry crust we use.

1. Heat the oven to 325°F. Roll out the dough to a 10-inch circle (see Variation, page 171). Lay it in a 9- or 10-inch springform pan and bake for 25 minutes or until lightly colored. Cool the crust on a rack.

2. Put the yolks in a large mixing bowl and stir them briefly with a fork, just until they're a homogenous, silky puddle of yellow. Add the cream cheese, ricotta, sugar, vanilla, and zests and, using a wooden spoon or a rubber spatula, beat the mixture until it's smooth and even. (You could also do this in a stand mixer with the paddle attachment—though you might want to use that mixer to whip your egg whites. Of course, you could whip the egg whites first, transfer them to another bowl, then cream the fats and sugar, and fold in the egg whites. Then again, you could be one of those people with an extra bowl for your mixer—in which case, good for you. You can make the machine do all the work. Or maybe you've got one of those handheld mixers. . . . Well, regardless of how you're outfitted, you'll need the fats and sugars creamed in one bowl—preferably the larger, if there's a choice—and stiff-whipped egg whites in another.)

3. Whip the egg whites with a whisk or electric mixer until they hold stiff peaks. Fold the egg whites into the cheese-yolk mixture. Usually

Serves 6 to 8

½ recipe
**Pâte Brisée
(recipe follows)**

**6 large eggs,
separated**

**Two 8-ounce
packages cream
cheese, at room
temperature**

**1 pound
(about 1 pint)
ricotta**

¾ cup sugar

**2 teaspoons pure
vanilla extract**

**Grated zest
of ½ lemon**

**Grated zest
of ½ orange**

the word "gently" comes into play in a recipe like this, but for this batter, you really need them integrated into the whole thing. Don't worry if you're deflating them; it's okay.

4. Pour the cheesecake batter into the prebaked crust and pop the pan into the oven. Bake the cheesecake for 1 hour. Turn off the oven and leave it in there for 1 hour more.

5. Refrigerate the cake until it's completely cooled. Remove the outer ring from the springform pan and, if you like, transfer the cheesecake to a serving platter. The cheesecake will keep for a couple days in the fridge, though it's unlikely it will last that long. Let it warm up a little from the fridge before serving.

PÂTE BRISÉE

Makes enough for two 10-inch tart shells or 2 cheesecake crusts or one of each

½ pound (2 sticks) unsalted butter, at room temperature

½ cup sugar

3 large egg yolks

1 large egg

Small pinch of fine sea salt

3⅓ cups (about 1 pound) all-purpose flour

1. Combine the butter and sugar in the bowl of a stand mixer fitted with the paddle attachment. Turn on the machine to a low speed and cream them together; if you start with room-temperature butter, it shouldn't take more than a few minutes. Add the egg yolks one at a time, letting each one be subsumed into the butter-sugar mixture before adding the next. With the mixer still running at low speed, add the whole egg and the salt. Once they've started to be incorporated, begin adding the flour, in three or four additions. Do not wait for the flour to be completely incorporated before adding more; just give it a few seconds to let it start to get to know the butter. Mix only until the dough has come together into a tacky, fatty, moist mass. It will be a messy beast to handle at this point, but do not overmix it—after a few hours in the fridge, it will be far more manageable.

2. Split the dough into two lumps, shape each one into a disk, and wrap them in plastic wrap. Chill for as long as possible: 2 or 3 hours is the bare minimum, 4 hours is preferable, overnight is ideal. Freeze one of the two if you don't need both; wrapped tightly, it will keep in the freezer for up to a month with no degradation in quality. (Thaw it in the refrigerator.)

3. Turn the oven to 325°F. Very, very lightly flour your counter or work surface and have a dish of flour close at hand for when things get sticky. Quickly roll out the chilled dough to a rough 12-inch round that's a little less than ⅛ inch thick. (The warmer and more worked the dough gets, the stickier it will be. If it's not rolling right, stop: put it on a baking sheet and put it in the freezer to chill. Have a beer, or take the dog for a walk. After 20 or 30 minutes, the dough will be more compliant. Keeping the butter cold is the key.)

4. If you're using a fluted tart pan, lay the tart dough in, pressing gently to nudge it into the flutes. If you're using a springform pan, cover the bottom and go up the sides a little, carefully fitting it into the pan. Bake for 25 minutes, or until it's lightly colored. Transfer to a rack to cool before filling.

CHEESECAKE CRUST VARIATION—Roll the dough out into a circle 10 inches or so in diameter, to cover the bottom of a 9- or 10-inch springform pan and go up the sides a little. Carefully fit it into the pan and bake as directed above.

CHOCOLATE TART

Stella d'Oro cookies weren't the best, but if you were growing up Italian in New York in the 1970s, they were a fixture: the anisette toast, the anisette sponge, the S-shaped cookie that doesn't taste like anything, and so on. Most were so-so cookies even to a kid, but there was a Swiss fudge variety, and when it showed up in the grocery bag, that was the best.

The Swiss fudge cookie was a round cookie base with a pool of chocolate in the center of it. This tart is an extrapolated adult rendition of a thumbprint cookie: a fine sugar dough crust filled with chocolate ganache, a refined version of a pleasure of youth.

One thing: "Make the tart dough and bake the tart shell" are nine words that represent a lot of time. So this tart takes a bit of planning. It is not a simple dessert you whip up after a day at the office. (That'd be the prunes recipe on page 168.)

Ostensibly serves 10

½ recipe Pâte
Brisée (page 170)

12 ounces
semisweet
chocolate chips

1½ cups
heavy cream

½ cup
granulated sugar

6 tablespoons cold
unsalted butter,
coarsely chopped

Powdered sugar
for dusting

1 cup heavy cream,
whipped
to soft peaks

1. Heat the oven to 325°F. Bake the dough in a 10-inch fluted tart pan as directed in Step 4 on page 171.

2. Put the chocolate chips in a large mixing bowl. Combine the cream and sugar in a medium saucepan and bring to a boil over medium-high heat, stirring constantly. Pull the pan from the heat and pour the contents over the chocolate. Let stand for a couple of minutes, then whisk well until the chocolate and cream are homogenized. Add the butter, whisking again until it has become part of the amalgamation.

3. Pour the ganache into the tart shell. Put the tart in the fridge and let it sit until the ganache is firm and set and sliceable—at least an hour, probably two. Serve the tart cool or cold, cut into wedges, with a dusting of powdered sugar and a plop of whipped cream.

Tiramisu

The magic of tiramisu is the mouthfeel—its weight and density and coldness. We crave the texture as much as the flavor.

1. *Make the soaking liquid:* Combine the coffee and 1 cup water in a small saucepan and bring it to a boil over high heat. When it boils, remove the pan from the heat and pass the coffee through a coffee filter. Let it cool to room temperature and then spike it with the rum. (Or purchase a 4-ounce cup of espresso— probably a double espresso—from your local coffee spot, bring it home—it doesn't need to be hot—dilute it with ½ cup water, and spike it with the rum.) Reserve until you're ready to assemble the tiramisu.

2. *Make the rum syrup:* Combine the sugar and water and in a small, heavy-bottomed saucepan and bring to a boil over medium-high heat. You can whisk it a bit at the beginning to help the sugar dissolve into the water, but once it comes to a boil, stop and let the sugar cook until it has taken on a deep amber color. At that point, pull the pan from the heat and add the cream in one big addition. Give the pan a little breathing room because the cream will bubble up rather furiously for a second. Then whisk, whisk, whisk until the sauce is smooth and even. Stir in the rum and let the sauce sit and cool while you get the mascarpone filling ready.

3. *Make the mascarpone filling, Part 1:* Whisk or, with an electric handheld mixer, beat the egg yolks and ¼ cup sugar together for a couple

Makes one 8-by-10-inch dish; serves 6 to 8

SOAKING LIQUID

5 tablespoons ground coffee

2½ cups water

2½ tablespoons Myers's dark rum

RUM SYRUP

1 cup sugar

1 tablespoon water

¼ cup plus 2 tablespoons heavy cream

2 tablespoons dark rum

(ingredients continued on next page)

MASCARPONE
FILLING

1 egg, separated

¼ cup sugar

**10 ounces
mascarpone,
chilled**

**⅓ cup plus
2 tablespoons very
cold heavy cream**

FOR FINISHING

**One 8-ounce
package ladyfingers
(or, in Italian,
savoiardi)**

**Cocoa powder
for dusting**

of minutes, until the mixture is thickened and pale yellow. Whisk in the mascarpone and reserve.

4. *Make the mascarpone filling, Part 2:* Whisk the heavy cream to stiff peaks and put it in the refrigerator. In another bowl, with a clean whisk (because any fat from the yolks or the cream will make whisking the egg whites impossible), beat the egg white until it holds soft peaks. Gently fold the whipped cream into the egg white, and then fold that mixture into the mascarpone mixture. Reserve.

5. *Build the tiramisu:* Start by dipping the ladyfingers one at a time into the rum-spiked coffee, dunking each one for 3 or 4 seconds. You want them cocktail-party tipsy, not frat-party drunk. Arrange them shoulder-to-shoulder in a single layer in the 8-by-10-inch rectangular dish. Drizzle half the rum syrup over the ladyfingers, pouring it freeform from a spoon. Use a spatula to gently disperse an even layer of the mascarpone filling over them, working gently so as not to rough them up. Do another layer: ladyfingers, syrup, mascarpone. Chill the tiramisu for at least 4 hours and as long as overnight. When you're ready to serve it, dust the top with the cocoa powder. Serve cold, with hot coffee.

TIRAMISU STRATA

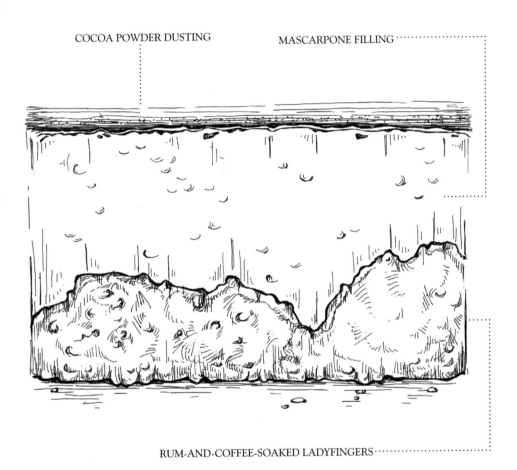

COCOA POWDER DUSTING

MASCARPONE FILLING

RUM-AND-COFFEE-SOAKED LADYFINGERS

HAZELNUT PANNA COTTA

Before the Spuntino, Falcinelli used to frequent a restaurant Sarah Jenkins used to run at 50 Carmine Street. He would order a plate or two of her hazelnut panna cotta. Every night. Sometimes twice a day. After his second or third hundredth serving, she told him how she made it. Whipped egg whites were the secret. That and Nutella.

At the Spuntino we do the Nutella but we don't mess with the egg whites, so there is even less work.

Serves 8

**2 packets
(1½ tablespoons)
unflavored gelatin**

**6 tablespoons
cold water**

4 cups heavy cream

**1 vanilla bean,
split lengthwise
and scraped**

1 cup Nutella

1. Stir the gelatin into the cold water in a small cup and let it soften while you scald the cream.

2. Put the cream in a medium saucepan over medium-low heat and bring it to the barest of simmers. Remove the pan from the heat and whisk in the vanilla and Nutella, mixing until the Nutella is dissolved into the cream. Let the mixture cool for 10 minutes, then whisk in the gelatin until dissolved.

3. Ladle the panna cotta base into eight ramekins or coffee cups or whatever individual-serving-size containers you have on hand: a smidge more than 4 ounces (½ cup) is the perfect size. Wrap the panna cottas individually in plastic and put them in the fridge to chill for at least 3 hours, or up to 2 days.

4. Serve the panna cotta straight from the fridge.

OLIVE OIL CAKE

It was a slippery slope with the olive oil. After we started importing our own, we were always finding new ways to use it. It was only so long before it went into a dessert.

Our olive oil cake works after a meal and is great for breakfast, but it's also ideal 3 P.M. pastry—not too sweet, not too heavy, great with a good espresso. Make sure to use a good-quality olive oil when making the cake; the fruit flavor of the olive is the thing you're trying to highlight.

Makes 6 mini Bundt cakes or one 10-inch cake

5 eggs

Zest of 1½ oranges

1¼ cups sugar

2 cups extra virgin olive oil

2 cups cake flour, sifted

1 teaspoon fine sea salt

1⅛ teaspoons baking powder

1. Heat the oven to 325°F. Combine the eggs, orange zest, and sugar in a stand mixer with the whisk attachment. Whisk on medium speed for a minute, until evenly mixed. Reduce the speed to low and add the olive oil in a slow, steady, continuous stream. Stir together the dry ingredients in a mixing bowl, then add the dry mixture to the egg mixture in three additions, whisking at low speed the entire time. Whisk just until the batter is smooth and even.

2. Rub the inside of the mini Bundt pans with a film of olive oil and fill with batter until the pan is nearly full. Bake the mini Bundts for 25 to 30 minutes, and the 10-inch cake for 45 to 50 minutes. The cake is done when a toothpick inserted into its thickest part comes out dry.

APPENDICES

I. Menus for Entertaining 181

    1. The Everyday Spuntino Menu 182

    2. Summertime Grilling 183

    3. Clam Night 188

    4. Brunch...192

II. Pairing Wines with Spuntino Food.....................194

III. Cheese at the Spuntino...202

IV. Frank Castronovo on Cooking with Kids...........209

V. How to Grow an Avocado Tree............................210

VI. How to Fillet Sardines 211

VII. The Frankies Calendar 212

APPENDIX I

MENUS FOR ENTERTAINING

The menu plans in this chapter are deliberately loose. Many are open-ended, with plenty of options and opt-outs built in. That's the way we roll. The thing you can't build into a menu is the company or the vibe, and those are the most important things. Honestly.

We've cooked in palaces of gastronomy and in hot spots where the only people who didn't have boldfaced names were those working in the kitchen. Great places. Great times. None of them were like this place, the Spuntino, where the food is easy and the times are good. Nobody's taking themselves too seriously, nobody's fussing over whether the wine's $100 or $10 a bottle, nobody's doing anything except getting together, breaking bread, and having a good time. You can do the same.

MENUS

1. THE EVERYDAY SPUNTINO MENU

2. SUMMERTIME GRILLING

3. CLAM NIGHT

4. BRUNCH

1. THE EVERYDAY SPUNTINO MENU

This is an easy dinner you can put together at the end of a long day: a three-course meal, mind you, which seems fancy, except that the first course is mostly store-bought and the dessert can be made in advance. Gnocchi or cavatelli are both easy enough to make and serve on the same night; otherwise, meatballs and a loaf of crusty bread will do just fine.

STARTER

Antipasto: See pages 25–53. Hit all your major antipasto food groups: olives (prepared as directed on page 28 or as you get them from the store), cheeses (pages 32–33), a couple of kinds of cured meats (pages 29–31), and a vegetable component (pages 34–45).

or

Salad: A big bowl of greens dressed with the Cipollini Onion Vinaigrette from page 70. Or, if you're feeling more energetic, any salad from pages 69–87.

MAIN COURSE

Cavatelli with Sausage & Browned Sage Butter (page 102)

or

Gnocchi Marinara with Fresh Ricotta (page 105)

or

Meatballs (page 124) with a loaf of crusty bread

DESSERT

Chocolate Tart (page 172)

or

Ricotta Cheesecake (page 169)

or

If it's a weeknight, just pick up something at the store or a bakery and serve it on nice plates. Sometimes it's the gesture more than anything else.

2. SUMMERTIME GRILLING

I don't know what winters are like where you live, but in New York, they're harsh. And long. And gray. So during the nicer months, we like to live outdoors as much as possible and involve a grill whenever we can.

Frankly, most of our barbecues aren't all that organized. Like most people, we gather some ground beef to make burgers, grill hot dogs, and throw a pile of peppers on the fire until they are soft and sweet. We're fine with lighter fluid and charcoal briquettes, though having a metal barbecue chimney to start the fire and some hardwood charcoal is always nice.

When we're more on the ball, a grill-out can last for hours. We start early, with just a few close collaborators, cooking vegetables on the grill instead of in the oven for antipasto. We sit around, sip something refreshing (it was ice-cold Lambrusco in the summer of '07, a chilly rosé from a winery called Bisson in '08, and a German pilsner called Einbecker in the summer of '09), and slowly start to build the meal. We shuck fava beans to snack on with chunks of Pecorino. Grilled meats are eaten later when guests arrive. We typically forget to replenish the fire and are forced to get it going again at least twice.

A menu for a good summertime hang would include some of the following:

MEAT
Sliced cold rib eye done on the grill is just about the greatest. The method is similar to the one on page 148; just skip the 375°F part—brown the meat out on the grill right when you start cooking, when the fire is good and hot, then finish it in a low oven indoors. Let it sit for as long as possible before slicing.

Italian sausages, just slicked with oil and grilled, are great, too. When we can get them, we go for the "pinwheel" sausages that are thinner than regular sausages (because they are stuffed into lamb intestines, not pig intestines) and coiled up like a snake. We like to grill them whole and serve them that way, cutting them up on a board at the table.

SEAFOOD

Castronovo's Cured Sardines (page 87) are killer off the barbecue. Just grill them for a minute or two on each side over a hot (but not smelting-hot) fire to give them a little color. Serve simply with lemon wedges. Grilled Squid (opposite) is also a must.

VEGETABLES

For salads, the Tomato, Avocado & Red Onion Salad (page 81) is a no-brainer. Add some Roasted Vegetable Salad (page 72).

FRANKIES LEMONADE

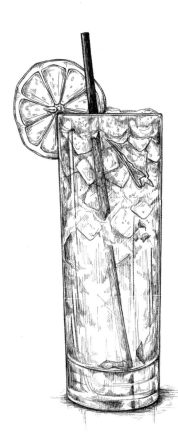

On hot days, we stir up cool batches of our own homemade lemonade.

Makes 1 tall glass

1 lemon

2 tablespoons agave nectar or simple syrup (50/50 water and sugar, heated until the sugar dissolves, and then stored in the refrigerator)

1 leafy mint sprig

1 cup ice cubes

Water or, preferably, sparkling water

Juice the lemon into a 16-ounce glass. Add the sweetener, mint, and ice. Stir or muddle, just so the ingredients in the glass get a chance to know one another. Top off with water. Repeat as necessary.

GRILLED SQUID

This is what the people we grew up around might call "calamar."

1. Get the fire in your grill atomic hot. In a large bowl, toss the cleaned squid in the chopped garlic and olive oil.

2. Grill the squid in batches so as not to crowd the grill. Know that they should take only about 60 to 90 seconds to cook, so have a clean bowl on hand for the cooked squid. When the first batch hits the heat, watch: like Ballpark Franks, they plump when you cook 'em. When they flail, flop, or wiggle, that means they're ready to get flipped over or removed from the grill to that bowl. The squid typically makes a bit of a mess of the grill grate; clean it with a stiff metal grill brush between batches (and right after the whole batch is done).

3. Hit the bowl of cooked squid with a couple of generous tablespoons of salt, then remove the hoods of the squid to a cutting board. Slice them into rings and return them to the bowl. Add the olive oil, parsley, and juice of 1 lemon. Toss well and taste. Add more salt, oil, and lemon as needed. Season heavily with black pepper and serve warm, or at whatever temperature it is outside.

Feeds about a dozen

5 pounds squid, cleaned (see box on page 186)

3 cloves garlic, finely chopped

½ cup olive oil, plus more as needed

Fine sea salt

¼ cup flat-leaf parsley leaves

The juice of at least 1 lemon, maybe 2

Lots of freshly ground black pepper

TO CLEAN SQUID

If your fish guy doesn't clean squid, here's what you do: Pull off the head, squeezing it above the eyes and pulling it away from the tentacles. Slide the cartilage—it feels and looks like a piece of thin clear plastic—out of the head. Give the inside of the head a good finger probing, and scoop out anything you find. Slip the thin mottled membrane off the hood (body) of the squid. Toss the membrane and rinse the hood.

Now turn your attention to the rest of the squid. Cut off the eyes and discard. Squeeze out the beak. Invert the tangle of legs so the beak, which is the hub at the center of that constellation of legs, is facing upward. Squeeze the body to pop it out, just like you pop the head off a dandelion. Discard the beak and rinse off the tentacles. Repeat with the remaining squid.

GRILLED VEGETABLES

Serves 6 or so; double for a crowd

1. Cut the eggplants and zucchini into pinky-thick slices. Cut the red onion into nice thick disks that won't fall apart on the grill. Core and seed the peppers and quarter them. Combine the vegetables, garlic, olive oil, and salt in a gigantic mixing bowl. Toss to coat the vegetables in the oil.

2. Grill over a medium-hot to kinda-getting-to-the-point-when-we-should-replenish-the-coals-hot fire for up to 45 minutes. Flip the vegetables a couple of times, until they are tender but not at all mushy. Pile up on a platter and serve warm or at ambient temperature.

2 meaty eggplants, with alternating vertical strips made by a vegetable peeler

2 each yellow and green zucchini

1 red onion

2 red, yellow, or orange bell peppers

4 cloves garlic, minced

1 cup olive oil

1 tablespoon salt

Frankies Corn Salad

Figure on 2 ears of corn per every 3 people.

Corn

Cherry tomatoes

Mint leaves

½ red onion

Olive oil

Juice of 1 lemon

Big pinch of salt

Pinch of red pepper flakes

Castelrosso cheese (optional)

This is always an improvised thing at a barbecue: because when corn and tomatoes are in season, it doesn't take much work to make them taste good.

1. Pull back the husks, remove the silk, and then pull the husks back over the cobs. Grill the corn for 5 minutes over a moderately hot fire; keep an eye on the ears in case the husks catch on fire.

2. Remove the corn from the grill, and when it's cool enough to handle, husk it. Cut the kernels off the cobs and put them in a big salad bowl.

3. Cut a pint's worth of cherry tomatoes in half (or a half-pint, or a single meaty heirloom, whatever looks good) and toss that in with the corn. Mint is nice here—maybe a couple of tablespoons of fresh mint leaves, torn. A half or a quarter of a red onion, diced, will add a good little pungent kick.

4. Then dress: Start with a couple of glugs of olive oil, the juice of a lemon, a big pinch of salt, and a pinch of red pepper flakes. Toss, taste, and adjust. See how easy that was? Castelrosso cheese, crumbled over the salad, is a nice touch.

3. CLAM NIGHT

In early summer, we put the clam pasta back on the menu.

And because shucking clams is a delicious mess, we always broil off a few extra dozen baked clams to reward ourselves—because what's the difference between shucking a couple of dozen and a dozen dozen? Once you're set up and have the hang of it, it's easy work.

SHUCKING CLAMS

Discard any clams with broken shells or with shells that don't fully close. If they're very sandy, place them one by one under running water, scrubbing the exterior of each with a brush, a kitchen towel, or even just your hand. Put the clams in a large bowl of cold water and ice to get them to "spit" any residual sand or silt. If they do spit out a lot of sand, change the water, rustle them up (gently), and wait another couple of minutes.

When you're ready to shuck them, grab the clams out of the bowl one at a time. Position the hinge end of the clam against the meaty part of the palm of your towel-draped "non-knife hand." Work over a widish bowl to collect the precious clam juice that will be a by-product of the shucking process. Sneak the thin blade of the clam knife in between the lips of the shell. (In moments of frustration, when he can't get the knife in, our friend Tony bangs an uptight clam against the counter to try and loosen it up. Professional? No. Effective? Often.) Once you've got the blade into the shell, draw it straight back toward the hinge, angling it toward the roof of the shell so you don't cut the meat in half. Pull it all the way back until the clam lets go of its hold on the shell.

Flip the shell open. Remove and discard the top shell, then use the knife to cut under the clam to free it from the shell. Put the loosened clam and its shell/holder on a baking sheet and repeat with the remaining clams.

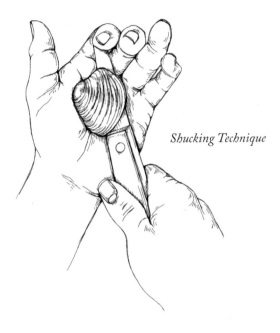

Shucking Technique

VARIATION—Don't want to shuck clams? Try this shortcut: Soak the clams in a big bowl of salted water for 10 minutes just before cooking them. The soak will give them a chance to spit out any sand they're holding on to. Drain them well. Before Step 2 of the Baked Clams recipe (page 190), add the whole clams and ¼ cup of liquid (water's fine, but white wine is better) and cover the pan for 4 or 5 minutes, by which point most of the clams should have popped open. Proceed with the recipe as directed, but be careful when doling out the dregs of the sauce from the pan—check it for sand or grit.

BAKED CLAMS

There is a school of steaming, shucking, chopping, and stuffing the clams back into their shells before baking them. We do not belong to that school.

Our ideal baked clam is a fresh, sweet clam as close to raw as possible, topped with bread crumbs that are as close to burnt as possible. The reality is usually a little bit between the two, but it's okay to dream.

To make them, we shuck the clams, leaving them on the half shell, top them with a seasoned bread-crumb mixture, apply olive oil liberally, and broil.

Serves 3 or 4

1¼ cups bread crumbs

2 tablespoons minced flat-leaf parsley

2 tablespoons minced fresh oregano

1 tablespoon grated Pecorino Romano or Parmigiano-Reggiano

1 clove garlic, minced

¼ cup olive oil, or as needed, plus more for drizzling

3 dozen littleneck clams, shucked (see page 188) and left in the bottom shells

Lemon wedges, for serving

1. Get the oven (or toaster oven) going until it's super-hot. Crank it up to its highest setting and keep it there, so it will really blast the bread crumbs with heat.

2. Mix the bread crumbs with the herbs, cheese, garlic, and olive oil in a medium bowl. Add more oil if necessary, mixing until the mixture has a texture like wet sand and an aroma like bottled Italian salad dressing.

3. Spoon the bread-crumb mixture onto the clams, using about 2 scant teaspoons per clam. You want them covered and coated, but you don't want to pack them. Do it loosely, lightly, and thoroughly. It's more tamping or topping than packing. (You're making baked clams, not snowballs.) Dribble a little olive oil over each clam to ensure the crumb topping is oiled and moistened and ready for the heat.

4. Bake the clams until the juices in the clam-shells are sizzling and the crumbs are browning, about 6 to 10 minutes. (Little black dots of burning crumbs signal that they're definitely ready.) Serve hot, with lemon wedges to help cool them down.

Spaghetti with Clams

This dish, like Tony Durazzo's Spaghetti with Crabs on page 118, is better over dried pasta than fresh. (We like very al dente linguine or spaghetti.) And though they're pretty, we prefer to ditch the shells. Picking around them as you're trying to wolf down a portion of pasta is just too much work.

Serves 4 (recipe is easily multiplied)

Fine sea salt

1 pound dried linguine or spaghetti

¼ cup olive oil

4 cloves garlic, smashed and finely chopped

Large pinch of red pepper flakes

1¼ cups just-shucked clams (about 2 dozen littlenecks) with the juice from shucking them

½ cup finely chopped flat-leaf parsley

Freshly ground black pepper

1. Put a large pot of water on to boil and salt it well.

2. Drop the pasta into the boiling water and get to work on the sauce: Put the olive oil in a wide skillet or sauté pan over medium-high heat. After a minute, add the garlic and cook it, stirring, for 2 to 3 minutes, until it's deeply golden but not yet browned. Add the red pepper flakes. Then add the clams and reserved clam juice and turn the heat down to medium-low. Let them simmer for 4 minutes or so until the pasta is ready.

3. Pull the pasta from the heat a minute or so earlier than its package indicates, drain it well, and put it on a large platter. Pour the clam sauce over the pasta and sprinkle with a pinch of salt and chopped parsley. Finish with lots of freshly ground black pepper at the table.

4. BRUNCH

We don't brunch. We weren't raised brunching. We were raised to go to church on Sundays and then go to Grandma's. But our customers love to brunch. And so we serve all the same stuff you can get at dinner and augment it with a few brunch items, including this recipe for French toast. Otherwise, you might as well have meatballs.

FRANKIES FRENCH TOAST

We've made two tweaks that we think take our French toast to the next level. The first is using real vanilla pods to flavor the soaking liquid. We warm and steep the seeds of the vanilla pod in cream and milk so they have a chance to blossom and bloom.

The other change is in the cooking technique: We flip frequently, every couple of minutes for 6 to 8 minutes. We also give the bread an additional layer of sugar with every flip, which envelops the toast in a crisp, thin caramel by the time it's done. The caramel-making process is kept in check by controlling the flame (keep it at medium heat) and by continuing to add butter, which reduces the temperature of the pan each time you add it.

1. Combine the eggs, cream, milk, and cinnamon in a mixing bowl. Scrape the seeds from the vanilla beans, add the seeds and beans to the cream mixture, and whisk until homogenized. Transfer the mixture to a saucepan and warm over medium heat until the mixture is very warm to the touch and the vanilla and cinnamon are aromatic. Let the mixture cool to room temperature, 20 to 30 minutes. (You can prepare this very early in the morning and hold it in the refrigerator for 3 or 4 hours.)

2. When you're ready to cook, pour the custard mixture into a wide shallow dish. Discard the vanilla beans.

Serves 3

5 large eggs

1 cup heavy cream

½ cup whole milk

Dash of ground cinnamon

2 vanilla beans, split

8 tablespoons (1 stick) butter (you may not use all of it)

3. Heat a tablespoon each of butter and oil in a 10-inch skillet over medium heat. (Or, even better, work two pans at the same time.) Dredge the bread in the custard mixture for a few seconds on each side—it should absorb some but not get soggy. Put it in the pan. After about 2 minutes, dust the top of the bread with a thin layer of confectioners' sugar and flip it over. Add a fillip of butter to the pan. Cook it for another 90 seconds to 2 minutes, then dust the side that's facing up, flip, and add a dot more butter. Repeat 2 or 3 more times, until both sides are covered in a caramel-brown crisp exterior. Remove from the pan and repeat for the remaining bread. Serve hot, with an excess of maple syrup available for passing.

¼ cup grapeseed oil

Six 1-inch-thick slices day-old bread

About ½ cup confectioners' sugar, or as needed

Maple syrup for serving

PAIRING WINES
WITH SPUNTINO FOOD

The first and only rule: buy enough wine. We stick to Italian wines at the Spuntino, but that's less important than having enough. When there's no bottom to the bottle, nobody minds what's in it.

Then it's time to figure out your strategy: one wine to get you through the night or a progression of wines to add an arc to the evening?

If you're going to serve only one kind of wine with a meal, it's best to go with an affordable crowd-pleaser. In most situations we'd choose a simpler red, like a Montepulciano; in the peak of the summer, we might do an all-rosé evening.

The multi-wine approach is harder to shop for, but only in that you have to push the cart to more stops while you're at the wine shop. We like to start with Lambrusco or prosecco—a glass of bubbly lightens everyone's spirit and goes well with nibbles early in the evening.

White wine is another option at this stage; if you've got enough people and enough time, you can chase bubbles with bianco.

Then it's vino rosso time. We like to do a progression of reds, from lighter wines, like Montepulciano, Pinot Nero, or Frappato and then move on to a bottle or two of bigger ones, like a Rosso di Montalcino, with the pasta and main courses. Obviously, how many wines make it along for the ride is dependent on how much your posse is in the mood to drink.

The following is basic advice about which types of grape to look for and how you can expect them to perform in the glass. We have generally avoided brand names, given how distribution varies from wineshop to wineshop even in our neighborhood.

BUBBLY WINE

Italy's marquee sparkling wine—and a significantly cheaper alternative to Champagne—is **prosecco**. It's bubbly, white, and usually about a third the price of the French stuff. Bigger brands can be flabby, but if you can develop a dialogue with a wineshop owner, you should be able to get your hands on a good bottle for not a lot of cash.

The sparkling wine we reach for more frequently is **Lambrusco,** a wine that got a bad name in the 1970s and 1980s when Riunite Lambrusco was served on ice. These days, boutique small-batch Lambruscos are easier to find and super-delicious. Lambrusco is fizzy, for the most part red (though it also comes in white and pink), and a little sweet. Ask your wine seller about sweetness: fruity sweet is good; candy sweet is not. It should be on the drier end of the spectrum.

WHITE WINE

In general, we like white wines from the north of Italy. Whites from the north have higher acidity and better structure (because of the region's higher altitudes and cooler temperatures) than wines from the south, which in our view tend toward fatness and flatness (though there are a million exceptions to that generalization).

The big three grapes to look out for:

FRIULANO

Unheard of in this country fifteen years ago, wines made from this grape, native to the Italian region of Friuli in the northeast, are some of the best values coming out of Italy today. Medium-bodied, aromatic, and with good acidity, they are a perfect match for salumi or any firm cheese from the north (in particular, Montasio).

GARGANEGA (SOAVE)

Garganega is the grape; Soave is the place. It is peachy wine, with a creamy, nutty flavor that will appeal to the Chardonnay drinker. In a wine scenario where you would be drinking two whites in a row, the Soave would come second. This wine goes great with buttery, creamy, and cheesy dishes.

PINOT GRIGIO

The truth about most Pinot Grigios, especially the cheap bottles and big brand names, is that they are terrible. But the grape didn't get to be popular without a history of quality. When you find a good one from a small producer, you'll be rewarded with a food-friendly, high-acidity wine that is floral and medium-bodied, with a ripe stone-fruit character.

PINK WINE

Pink wine—which we call rosé even if rosato is the proper Italian way to refer to it—is warm-weather wine. It is our go-to party fuel during the summer, served cold and in large quantities. Very, very few pink wines benefit from any aging, and none that do are from Italy. As such, you want to buy a rosé that is no more than a year old.

Rosés are books that are easily judged by their covers. They are typically bottled in clear glass, so it is easy to peg where on the color wheel they land—salmon pink to strawberry red. And the color will tell you most of the wine's story: Want something light and mineraly? Look for the nursery pink stuff. Fruitier and fuller? Look for the reddest of the batch. Start experimenting early in the summer, find the one that's going to be your wine for that summer, and buy it by the case.

RED WINES

As a rule, northern Italian red wines are more sophisticated, structured, and acidic; southern Italian red wines are fuller-bodied, fruit-driven, and fun.

EVERYDAY RED WINES

MONTEPULCIANO
Our go-to everyday choice for red is Montepulciano d'Abruzzo: Montepulciano is the grape, Abruzzo is the place. It's a crowd-pleaser that's medium- to full-bodied, agreeably tannic and with a dark berry flavor, plus a hint of barnyard and a strong minerality. There's a lot of it out there that is delicious and cheap, so get it while the getting is good.

NERO D'AVOLA
Nero d'Avola, a Sicilian grape, makes a Sicilian wine of the same name. It's a close relative of Syrah. It makes fruity wines—blueberry isn't uncommon—with a smoky mineral accent derived from the volcanic Sicilian soil. It's low tannin, often (but not always) low acid, and medium-bodied, so it plays nice with salads and doesn't try to compete with the tomato sauce on meatballs or braciola.

PRIMITIVO
Primitivo is Zinfandel's Italian doppelgänger. It starts out super-fruity with a raisinish bent, and then a brash and brambly specter chases the fruit. Primitivo really likes to be served cold, and goes well with meat and grilled anything. It doesn't mix well with raw vegetables or young cheeses.

BARBERA
Barbera and Dolcetto are affordable wines from the dependable Piedmont region of Italy; if we were choosing, we'd pick Barbera, usually one from Asti

or Alba. Some producers use very traditional methods and come up with rustic, lighter wines; others aim for a fruit-forward, oakier style. In either case, the textbook profile is luscious and medium- to full-bodied, with blackberry, violet, and flower notes dominating. Traditional styles will have little tannin; modern bottlings will have more. Either style is acidic enough to drink with almost any food.

SANGIOVESE

Sangiovese is one of the most widely planted grapes in Italy, and the results range from the cheapest straw-wrapped bottles to some of the country's grandest and most expensive wines. On the affordable and more quaffable side, look for Chianti Classico. (The "classico" thing is not about how classic the wine is—though, seeing as that it's been made for centuries, it's pretty damn classic—but about the wine being from a specific subregion within the sprawling Chianti district.) Chianti Classicos, like many Sangiovese-based wines, are marked by cherry fruit flavors—usually tart or dark cherry—and notes of leather and tobacco.

While you're on the Sangiovese hunt, be on the lookout for a wine called Rosso di Montalcino, made from Sangiovese (actually from a cousin called Sangiovese Grosso) and grown a bit south of the Chianti area on the plateau around the town of Montalcino in Tuscany. The grand wine from there is Brunello di Montalcino, and it's one of the greatest wines in the world. Trouble is, it needs years to relax and unwind in the bottle before it's at all approachable in the glass. (When it does wind down, it has a guttural earthiness, a Burgundian barnyard funk, and a tightly wound, hard-won core of amazing cherry fruit overlaid with saddle leather.) But its little brother, Rosso di Montalcino, isn't a sulky second-run wine by any stretch: it is where it's at. You spend less money and get a wine you can drink right now. It goes well with any kind of food, particularly meats, and anything with tomato sauce.

NEBBIOLO

Wines made from the Nebbiolo grape—named after the fog, *nébbia*, that frequently envelops the steep hills of Piedmont in northwestern Italy—come in a huge range of styles. The fruit can be fresh or dry cherry; floral notes can be rose or violet; and many have deeper, funkier tarlike notes. Most bottles labeled Nebbiolo should be affordable and drinkable right now. The grape is also the chief constituent of Barolo and Barbaresco—two of Italy's (and the world's) greatest wines. Neither drinks well in its youth, and both tend to get very expensive very quickly. If you can afford them, especially from vintages that have had a few years to age, you'll find that there are few wines that drink better or offer more pleasure.

HARDER-TO-FIND-BUT-TOTALLY-WORTHWHILE WINES FROM NORTHEASTERN ITALY

This is an exciting time for Italian wine in America, with products from small wineries finding their way onto store shelves. We get the most excited by wines coming out of the northeastern part of Italy, particularly Friuli and Alto Adige. A few good reds are:

SCHIOPETTINO
A fuller-bodied red wine that still manages to be brisk. It's got a dark cherry fruit character to it, but with muskier notes like white pepper or tobacco. File under "friend of pork" and serve when you're going to lay out a bunch of salumi or make the Braised Pork Shank (page 143) or Sausage with Peppers & Onions (page 134).

REFROSCO
Refrosco is medium- to-full bodied, purple, and food-friendly, for the most part. Even when the grape goes into making a rosé—and some of our favorite pink wines are made from the Refrosco grape—the wine is always marked by juicy red fruit and a hint of violet.

SCHIAVA
The name means "little slave girl," a frankly offensive term that refers to how easy it is for winemakers to manipulate and grow it out in the fields. (Hey, we didn't name it.) The wine is soft, light, and distinguished by woodsy and smoky notes. We like it chilled down as an aperitivo. It's very good with cheeses and salumi.

And we like one white in particular:

RIBOLLA GIALLA
Popular in northeastern Italy and across the border in Slovenia (where it is also made into some killer wines, particularly by a winemaker named Stanislao

Radikon), it is what we call a farmhouse wine. It's medium- to full-bodied, golden in color, and marked by an intensely aromatic nose (honeysuckle comes to mind) and a nutty flavor on the palate. Ribolla is a natural partner for younger, firmer cheeses.

THE HOT & COLD OF IT

Let's all agree on something: Warm wine sucks. Right? You've experienced it somewhere: a friend's house, a careless restaurant, at home after forgetting you put the wine on top of the fridge, not in it. In the glass, it's what wine geeks call "fat"—meaning sloppy and not zippy. It's also more likely to taste like what wine nerds define as "hot"—meaning the alcohol gets stirred up and is more noticeable and less integrated.

All red wines benefit from a chill. They should be served at 55 to 60°F, which means that when you grab the bottle (probably from the fridge), it should feel cooler than the room. Our rule is: whatever the wine, chill it a bit. And honestly, if we were serving cheaper red wines, say those from $12 to $15, at home, we would serve them refrigerator cold. Wine can always warm up, but the last thing you want to be doing is reaching for an ice cube.

TRAVIS'S MULLED WINE

During the winter, we always have a pot of Travis's Mulled Wine going on the bar. Travis Kauffman, our manager, came up with this recipe as the perfect starter drink to help thaw out just-arrived guests. The aroma fills the room with the essence of wintertime entertaining.

One 750-ml bottle red wine

1 cup sugar

3 cinnamon sticks

A few strips of lemon and orange zest, cut from the fruit with a vegetable peeler, avoiding the white pith

3 cloves

Combine all the ingredients in a saucepan and heat over low heat just until nearly hot to the touch. Never boil the wine, and remove and discard the spices after 30 minutes. Serve at once, or let steep off the heat and then gently rewarm to serve.

MIX IT UP

• *Add a whole star anise or a few cardamom pods to the mix.*

• *Add a shot of grappa to each mug (off the heat, just before serving).*

• *Make mulled cider: Use apple cider in place of the wine.*

• *Make hot buttered rum: Use apple cider in place of the wine and stir a tablespoon of butter into each 8-ounce mug; add a shot of rum just before serving. It's like a mug of alcoholic hot apple pie.*

APPENDIX III

CHEESE AT THE SPUNTINO

Italian cheeses rule the roost at Frankies. Our favorite cheeses for the antipasto hour—or really anytime—are the fresh ones like mozzarella and burrata. They're even better dressed with olive oil and served with good crusty bread. After that, it's sheep's milk cheeses (including Pecorino Romano, the stalwart, go-to cheese of our kitchen), then cow's milk cheeses and then Italian goat's milk cheeses. Our favorites are described here. See page 32 for ideas on how to put together the right selection of cheeses for your dinner.

MOZZARELLA & ITS COUSINS

A fundamental truth: everyone loves **mozzarella**. People who don't know anything about cheese love it. Even people who don't like cheese like mozzarella.

And the best mozzarella is the freshest mozzarella. Unlike drier and firmer cheeses—cheeses that rely on aging to develop their flavor and texture—the flavor of mozzarella begins to decline a few days after it's made. It's not a huge drop-off, but there's a perceptible loss of the sweet, creamy milk flavor and often an intensification of a sourness that should be a faint background note.

The good news is that mozzarella can be made anywhere and should be made everywhere; so getting your hands on some fresh product shouldn't be too much of a strain. Any good Italian deli is going to make its own—the mozzarella from Caputo's, an Italian deli in Carroll Gardens, is still warm when we buy it—or get it from someplace nearby that does. National brands like Polly-O and Calabria— they're suitable for melting on something, but even then they're a last resort.

Fresh Mozzarella

The step up from regular mozzarella is **mozzarella di bufala**—the real thing, from Campania, made from the milk of water buffalo. These days many good Italian food shops are bringing it in. The really good stuff is expensive, in part because it gets jetted over here from Italy.

That's our favorite time to eat buffalo milk mozzarella, on the day we get our delivery from the airport. It's so fresh that when you open the package, you release that fresh puff of Italian air that the cheese got put in there with. So good. Water buffalos are different from cows. They eat other things than the cows that make domestic mozzarella eat, and the nuances of the Italian stuff are insane.

And then there are two harder-to-find relatives of mozzarella from the province of Puglia that are worth seeking out: **burrata** and **stracciatella**.

Burrata is still a bit hard to find in the States, but if you have access to a good cheese shop and ask for it, they should be able to track some down for you. To make burrata, cheese makers take a sheet of curd that has been pulled to the texture of mozzarella and wrap it around a nearly liquid mixture of thickened cream and silky strands of barely pulled cheese curd. They twist the sheet of firmer cheese closed, forming a ball with a topknot, and fasten it shut with a green leaf. The finished cheese is a like a cream-filled mozzarella water balloon. We like to bring a whole lobe of it to the table, slice it open, and let the people we're feeding see the milky liquid cheese spill out. Hit it with a splash of olive oil and a little salt and pepper, put some bread out, and watch it disappear.

The name of that sweet milky liquid used to fill the burrata is stracciatella, and we've recently started to see tubs of it for sale here in New York. It doesn't hold together or have a cheeselike shape or appearance: It's a tub of cream interspersed with delicate shreds of a mozzarella-like nature.

It's the sort of thing that's probably bought in secrecy and eaten alone, with a loaf of bread and a bottle of olive oil. It's almost too good to share— like a chance to mainline the very essence of a fresh Italian cheese.

SHEEP

Pecorino Romano is a sheep's milk (or, specifically, ewe's milk, but that's hard to tell someone on a Saturday night in a busy restaurant) cheese. We go through more Pecorino Romano than any other cheese at the Spuntino.

This cheese has a millennia of tradition behind it. It was a Roman cheese, and it was then and is now produced in strongholds of the old Roman empire: Lazio, the region that's home to Rome; the southern reaches of Tuscany; and, west, across the Tyrrhenian Sea, the sheep-friendly island of Sardinia. Sardinia is where most Pecorino Romano is produced today.

The cheese is dry, dense, and salty with an animally funk. We find it indispensable in the kitchen as an ingredient. It goes in meatballs, braciola, and most of our pastas. It adds a depth and a kind of savory saltiness we can't get otherwise. It's a perfect complement to the pungency of white pepper, and it's so affordable that it's the only cheese we cook with.

Pecorino Romano's only fault is that it doesn't fare well as an eating cheese—better to serve a younger, less salty Pecorino, like the two described below, instead. Store Pecorino Romano tightly wrapped in the fridge, where it will keep for months but is best used within two weeks. Save the rinds for cheese broth (see page 14).

Il Re del Pecorino is an aged sheep's milk cheese from Florence. It's crumbly and sharp; its saltiness and butteriness come together in a buttered-popcorn-like flavor. Pecorino Romano is the everyman's sheep cheese, and this one is the king: "Il Re." You could buy a two-pound chunk of it, put it out at a party with a couple of knives, and basically be done with it.

Formaggio di Fossa is like a cheese that was kidnapped: after a couple of months of aging in the orderly cheese factory, this sheep's milk cheese gets stuffed into a bag and hidden in a subterranean pit. (*Fossa* translates to cave or crypt.) This happens in a place called Sogliano al Rubicone, in Emilia-Romagna. After five months, on the day of the feast of St. Catherine, the cheesemakers show pity and bring the cheese back to the factory to regain its composure and shape before shuttling it out of the country and selling it to two guys with the same name in Brooklyn.

Formaggio di Fossa has a golden hue and a firm texture. It is nutty, dryish, and flaky, with fruity overtones to its salty sheepiness and a particular funkiness attributable to its time in captivity. Honey-drizzled walnuts are a good accompaniment.

COW

PROVOLONE

Provolone is a stalwart of every Italian-American cheese shop we've ever been to: those huge columns of cheese, yellow like old bones, stamped with red logos, suspended from the ceiling by thick ropes, giving the whole shop that characteristic Italian-cheese-shop smell, and slowly, slowly, here and there, dripping a trickle of fat down onto the counters and floor as the cheese ages and sharpens.

Originally a southern Italian cheese (production shifted to the Po Valley in northern Italy about a century ago), provolone is still the eating cheese of choice for many Italian Americans with roots in Naples and Sicily.

Provolone is sold in countless shapes—those tall pillars, little globes, bells, cows, and more—but the shape matters less than the provenance: make sure you're getting Italian provolone, not any of the very similarly packaged stuff produced in America, which is less complex and nuanced. It shouldn't be hard to find the Auricchio variety we use at the Spuntino; Auricchio is a giant in the provolone business.

We prefer regular provolone, sometimes called *provolone dolce. Provolone piccante,* which is older and sharper, is a good cheese, but regular old provolone—younger and mellower—is what we grew up on and what we use at the Spuntino. (Provolone piccante is also different in that it's made with strong-tasting sheep's or goat's rennet—an enzyme from the animals' stomachs that is essential to curding—while the dolce is made with calf's rennet, which results in a sweeter, milder cheese.)

MONTASIO

Montasio, from the northeastern provinces of Friuli–Venezia Giulia and the Veneto, is a crowd pleaser if there ever was one. Firm yet just soft enough to the bite with a subtle, appealing creaminess, it was one of the first cheeses on our original list, and it still holds a place in our hearts. People love to add it to the Roasted Vegetable Sandwich (page 57).

CASTELROSSO

Castelrosso is a cheese from Piedmont with a cool texture. It willingly crumbles into little clods that are perfect for nibbling on or sprinkling over a salad (We use it in our Shaved Raw Brussels Sprouts on page 74.) It's aged for only a couple of months, so it still has a very fresh, sweet milk flavor. It finishes with gentle saltiness and refreshing tang.

ROBIOLA BOSINA

On the label of the robiola we buy there's a cute, almost childish drawing of a pastoral scene—a spotted cow and a shaggy sheep hanging out by a river in the mountains—that gets across the pertinent info about where the milk is from and where the cheese is made. It's a softish, pastelike cheese with a natural bloom of white powder on it. It's primarily clean, bright, and grassy, but woodsy/earthy flavors add a note that make it a serious cheese.

GENERAL TRENDS IN ITALIAN WINE REGIONALITY

CHEESE REFERENCE

NORTH {
light
acidic
minerally
refined
}

MONTASIO—*Friuli*
Semi-firm, Nutty & Mild

↕ ACID (+/-)

PROVOLONE—*Veneto*
Semi-firm & Sharp

NEBBIOLO

TALEGGIO—*Lombardia*
Soft & Stinky

BARBERA

↕ FRUIT (-/+)

ROBIOLA BOSINA—*Piemonte*
Soft, Buttery & Grassy

SANGIOVESE

CASTELROSSO—*Piemonte*
Crumbly & Grassy

CENTRAL {
medium-full
balanced
earthy
fruit driven
}

GORGONZOLA—*Emilia-Romagna*
Semi-soft, Blue & Pungent

↕ SUN (-/+)

FORMAGGIO DI FOSSA—*Emilia-Romagna*
Firm, Racy & Earthy

MONTEPULCIANO

IL RE DEL PECORINO—*Toscana*
Firm, Sheepy & Sharp

PRIMITIVO

↕ AVERAGE TEMPERATURE (-/+)

BURRATA AND STRACCIATELLA—*Puglia*
Soft, Decadent & Creamy

SOUTHERN & ISLANDS {
full-bodied
low acid/soft
rustic
ripe
}

MOZZARELLA DI BUFALA—*Campania*
Soft, Milky & Fresh. Perfect.

NERO D'AVOLA

PECORINO ROMANO—*Sardegna*
Firm & Salty. Cheese for grating.

↕ DAYS IN GROWING SEASON (-/+)

AMALATTEA—*Sardegna*
Semi-firm & Nutty

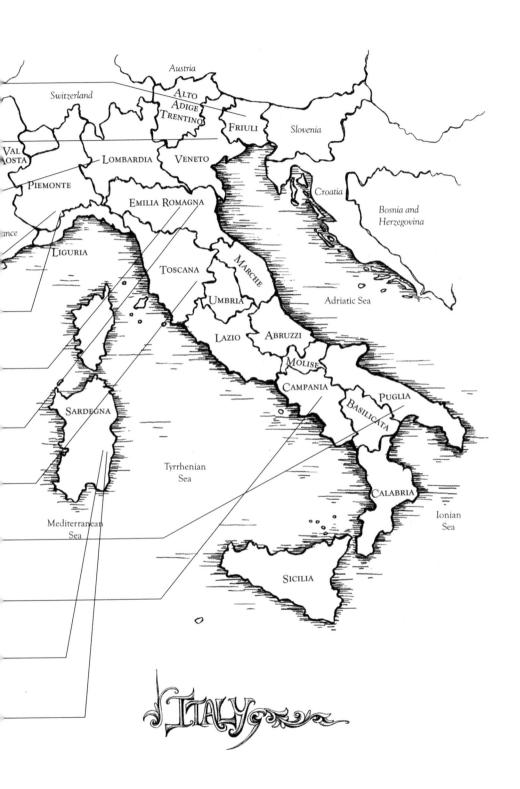

Austria

Switzerland

ALTO
ADIGE
TRENTINO

FRIULI

Slovenia

VAL
AOSTA

LOMBARDIA

VENETO

PIEMONTE

ance

EMILIA ROMAGNA

Croatia

Bosnia and
Herzegovina

LIGURIA

TOSCANA

MARCHE

UMBRIA

Adriatic Sea

LAZIO

ABRUZZI

MOLISE

CAMPANIA

PUGLIA

BASILICATA

SARDEGNA

Tyrrhenian
Sea

CALABRIA

Ionian
Sea

Mediterranean
Sea

SICILIA

ITALY

GORGONZOLA

Gorgonzola is the go-to blue in the Italian kitchen, the analogue to Roquefort in France and Maytag Blue in America. It's buttery, sweet, and full-flavored, as a raw-milk cheese should be, and the blue veins that run through it are pungent and sharp.

TALEGGIO

Taleggio is a big, square cow's milk cheese from Lombardia, with a soft, pale-rust-colored rind wrapped around a dense, pasty brick of stinky cheese. We find it to be too strong on its own, so we serve it with honey and walnuts. Make sure to give any Taleggio you buy a good sniff beforehand; it progresses from a mellow stink when it gets off the boat to an ammoniated, drippy mess toward the end of its days. We vastly prefer it on the mellower side, though we have been known to take past-its-prime overripe Taleggio and melt it on toast with tomato and onion.

GOAT

We don't do much with Italian goat cheeses. Our favorites are the fresh ones—the type most often labeled *chèvre* in this country—and there aren't a lot of those coming over from Italy. Besides, they wouldn't be as fresh as the domestic product we could get anyway.

The one glorious exception to that rule is Amalattea, a golden-colored Sardinian goat cheese that's aged for 3 months. It's on the dryish side of the semi-firm cheese spectrum, and it tastes sweet, with a nutty, mellow creaminess and floral finish. Great stuff.

APPENDIX IV

FRANK CASTRONOVO ON COOKING WITH KIDS

Cooking with your kids means cooking at home, cooking from scratch, sitting down together, and sharing a meal—and what could be more important than that? The great thing about involving your children in cooking is that it teaches them all kinds of skills, like organization and responsibility, while helping you—the parent—with some of your own, namely patience.

It's not like at the restaurant, where there's a guy who needs the job and wants to learn. Sometimes kids want to help more than anything in the world—for about five minutes. You get them started, and then suddenly it's even more important to chase the dog around the apartment—and off they go.

But over the years my daughters, Sophie and Louise, have become increasingly helpful in the kitchen. My wife and I don't even think about making a vinaigrette for the dinner salad; Sophie is on it. I've taken the time to teach her how to taste. "Does it need more salt? Does it need more vinegar?" And so, though she is only seven, she already knows to taste food for seasoning before serving it. There are plenty of adults who don't know how to do that.

The ground rule that I emphasize to my girls is that the kitchen is a place to be respected. There's heat, and there are sharp objects. One can get hurt. I always supervise anything that involves using knives or the stove (even stirring a slowly simmering pot of the Sunday sauce. If it tips over, you don't want them in the way of that tomato volcano). It may sound counterintuitive, but sharp knives are the safest knives to work with: dull knives slip off tomatoes and into fingers, sharp knives cut smoothly. (See page 5 for knife sharpening tips.) If you're not going to sharpen your knives regularly, don't let your kids work with them.

A few of my favorite things to do with my kids:

- Shaping fresh pastas, particularly cavatelli and gnocchi, and stuffing ravioli
- Making Meatballs (see page 124) and topping Crostini (see page 46)
- Layering Eggplant Marinara (see page 137) or lasagna (see page 164)
- Pitching in with Vegetable Antipasti (see pages 34–45): If you've trained your kids to wash and simply prepare vegetables, you've given them a lifelong skill.

APPENDIX V

HOW TO GROW AN AVOCADO TREE

Avocados have pits. Avocado pits can be grown into avocado trees. Avocado trees are nice to have around the house. So, if you're eating avocados and you don't live in a cave, why not try to grow one?

Pretty much everybody in the Spuntinoverse has grown an avocado tree at some point. It's just one of those weird things that you end up doing if you spend enough time listening to old LPs in rooms filled with macramé.

TO TRY IT

Rinse off any avocado flesh from the seed, spike it with three toothpicks around its middle, and suspend the fatter end in a Mason jar filled with enough water to come about one-third of the way up the seed. Put it on the windowsill and replenish or change the water as need be.

When the sprout reaches about half a foot in height, cut it back to just a few inches. Wait patiently.

Assuming you've gotten this far—the roots are living and the sprout is growing—transfer the plant to a pot filled with soil, leaving the top half of the pit, from which the sprout is shooting, exposed. Keep it in the sunlight. Water periodically. With a green thumb and some luck, you'll get an avocado tree that will last you for years.

APPENDIX VI

HOW TO FILLET SARDINES

If your fishmonger won't help you with the fish cleaning (and we do understand what you're going through if he doesn't), you've got to do it yourself. It's a little messy but nothing to fret about. First, clean your sink and put a cutting board in it. That's where you'll be working. (It's a basin, so it will catch errant scales flying away or any other mess that's made.) To gut the fish, cut it open down the belly, from where the head meets the beginning of the body all the way to the tail fin. Use an incision that's just deep enough to get through the skin. Scoop out the innards. Discard that stuff and rinse out the fish. Repeat for the remaining sardines.

To scale the fish, hold it down against the board by its tail and scrape off the scales: it's not quite scraping, actually—all you need to do is drag a spoon or the back of a knife against the "grain" of the scales, from the tail toward the head. They'll come right off (and probably fly everywhere, which is why you're working in the sink). Check your work to make sure the fish is clean of all scales by running your finger over the skin, then rinse the fish.

Filleting time: super-easy. Flop the fish onto its back. Starting right behind the head, use your fingers to splay the cut-open fish out like a book from head to tail. Get a firm grasp on the head and gently lift it up; the spine will follow. Look over the flesh for any big bones that were left behind (tiny ones are fine—don't drive yourself nuts). Cut off the tail, cut the fish in half down the line where the backbone used to hold it together (assuming that it hasn't come apart already), and rinse.

Voilà: filleted fish. Use as directed on page 87.

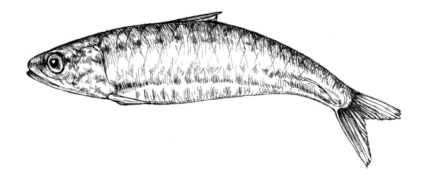

APPENDIX VII

THE FRANKIES CALENDAR

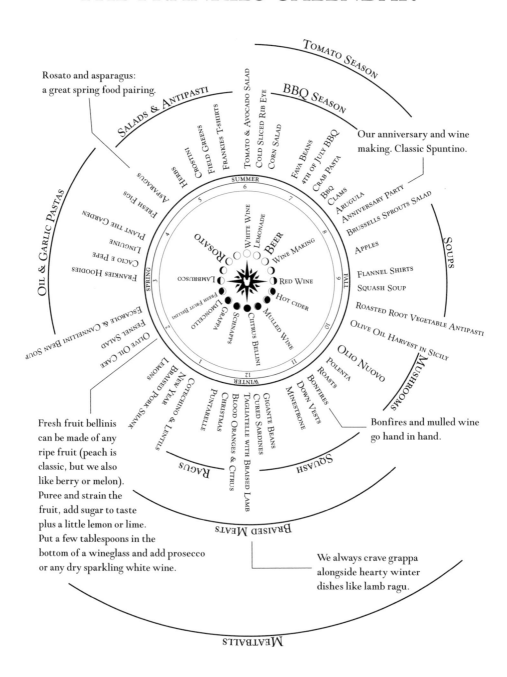

Rosato and asparagus: a great spring food pairing.

Our anniversary and wine making. Classic Spuntino.

Fresh fruit bellinis can be made of any ripe fruit (peach is classic, but we also like berry or melon). Puree and strain the fruit, add sugar to taste plus a little lemon or lime. Put a few tablespoons in the bottom of a wineglass and add prosecco or any dry sparkling white wine.

Bonfires and mulled wine go hand in hand.

We always crave grappa alongside hearty winter dishes like lamb ragu.

ACKNOWLEDGMENTS

FRANK FALCINELLI

I'd like to give the following thanks:

To the Falcinellis, the De Marches, the Martuccis, and the Vallefuocos for the courage to move to a new land and stick it out so that their kids and grandchildren could have the opportunity of a better life in America and New York City.

Super thanks to our customers: the first-timers, the regulars, and the lifers. You are an amazing audience. We love you.

To the entire staff of Frankies Spuntino, front of the house and back of the house, past and present: you make it all happen and not a day goes by that we don't appreciate it.

Extra-special thanks to Travis Kauffman for his optimism, inspiration, and creative force. And thanks for teaching Merlin to be the man.

To Tony Durazzo for being the kid from President Street who became a man of the world, and for sharing his wisdom with all of us every day (Go, Brooklyn Tech!).

To Peter Meehan for taking two voices and an idea and making it look easy. Grace under pressure.

To my partner Frank Castronovo, a great chef and an even better accomplice in creation, who stepped out of yesterday and into a world we created together from our imaginations and our histories.

I am grateful to:

Merlin

Frank and Marie, Vincent, Lisa and
 Jimmy

Emily, Olivia, and Francesca

Otto and Ann, Germano and
 Francesca

The Lappins

The Covingtons, Binkorowskis, and
 Falcones

The Ronan family

220th Street

Martin Van Buren HS

Heinz and Jens

Patrick Pinon

The faculty of the Culinary Institute
 of America

André and Ariane Daguin

Dominic Toulousy

Michel Guérard

JL

Auch

Bacchus

Gil Moglia

Greg Alauzen

Guy Cerina

Jimmy Henderson

Charlie Palmer

David Burke

Don Pintabona

Drew Nieporent

Eric Ripert

Laurie Mulstay

Jen Doyle

Lola

Mike Meehan

Alan Wexler

D. Cole Frates

Darren A

The Vetiver family

Farmer Dave

p baltz

The Black Crowes family: amy, cutlets, rr, sven, luther, adam, steve

Chris and Allison, Cheyenne and Ryder

The Corbin family

Greg Fanslau

Rolf

Zac and the Posen family

Zach

Bruce Wexler

Kate

Santo

The Kirkes

Nikolich and Rebecca

d pittman

Duane Sorenson and the Stumptown family

Jerry G

New Riders

Lonesome cowboy

Carmine C and Eddy F

Bev

Tommaso and the Partanna family

d. Sherry

Stella

Rene

Jacqueline

Kevin and the OGT family

Nancy Luquer

Amber Clapp

Julian

Kevin & Maite

The McKean family

The Kaminskys

Sunny

Neil Young and Crazy Horse

Bob Dylan and the Band

Chris Hillman

Marmaduke and the Byrds

CSN

Waylon Jennings

Jon Feldman

Neal Jacobs

Marci DeLozier Haas

Andrew Kesselring

RVW

Fiona

Declan

KW

The Golden Heart

Rob and Robin

Robin and Steven

Jack and Eileen

Troop 332

RdR

Francesco, Alba, Chiara, and Nina Clemente

Micah Finkle

Will Prunty and Luigi

Crispo

T. Dideo

The Artisan family: Ann Bramson,
    Ingrid Abramovitch, Peter
    Workman

Kim Witherspoon

The Sonic Youth family

Santi

Dustin and Jackie Yellin

Billy Kent

Jean-Georges

Ricardo and the Sciuto family

HP

Spuntinoman

The Volpe family

Mikey Pipes

Frank Dank

Joe Rock

The Bamundos

Our Lady of Lourdes QV

Dennie Goglielmo

Michael "fellow man of letters"
    Thomas

Russ R

Dana Cowin

Kate Krader

Dave C & Momo Ssäm for the grub

San Sebastian, Spain

John Fahey

Michael Klausman

Gurus Galore

Phil Lesh and the Grateful Dead
    family

Nozawa

Alain Ducasse

André Soltner

Jean-Jacques Rachou

DB

Alan and the Kamco family

Adam Chodos

Ali Pratt

Antonio Guardinino

Shane Welch

Vito

PJ

Sifton

Muhlke & Strand

Hannah

Hazel J

Christina, Andrew and Julep

Antonio Andolini

Queens Village

Mathieu Motorino

Thomas Keller

Amsterdam

Dr. Steve Guggino

Greg Ronan

Amed

Special thanks to all of the staff of
    17 Clinton St., Prime Meats and
    Café Pedlar

You have all been sources of great inspiration on our journey.

In loving memory of Jeanine, Ann, Christine, Lou, Mary, Freddy, Jim,
    Francesca, Germano, George

If there is anyone we have forgotten, we sincerely apologize, and thank you.

FRANK CASTRONOVO

To my girls Heike, Louise, and Sophie. You are the sunshine of my life.

I would also like to thank:

Mom and Dad.

LDL (Ahmed)—my mentor.

The Dileos of Humboldt Street: Carmella, Lucia, Louis, and Philomena (you left us too early, but you're still in my heart).

The Castronovos, 13 Pine Street, Pearl Harbor Frank, Aunt Sue & Heather, Mary, Annie, and Alfred.

The Muscarellas. Anthony, my little brother. The Grossos, Lutzs, Nastris, Karatzs, Chestaros, Aunt Joann and Dave, Elizabeth and Jennifer.

The Costellos (Donald, Bobby, Patricia, Ma, and Clancy: you took me in and gave me what I needed when I needed it). I will never forget QV.

The Leonards: Joe, Jimmy, Lorna, and Julie.

My teenaged home away from home: the Boy Scouts of America Troop 158, Our Lady of Lourdes, P.S. 33, L.I. Tomahawks football, Bobby Tavares, Jeff Schoen, John Gunther, Borkel Place, Alley Pond Park skateboarding, WLIR, P.S. 18 handball, Elmont Junior Hockey, Elmont Memorial teachers and coaches (football & lacrosse), the New York Islanders hockey dynasty, 1980–1984.

Richard Poslet, who inspired me to be a chef at the age of fifteen.

Jerry Durso, my first and coolest boss. God bless you.

The French chefs who refined my cooking; RTR, Willy Krause, Romeo DeGobbi, Christer Larsson, Paul Bocuse, Jean Fleury, Roger Jaloux, Christian Bouvarel, Bernachon, Eric Pansu, David Bouley, Jean-Claude Iacovelli, Drew, JG Vongerichten, Eric Ripert, Eckart Witzigmann, Bernard Guth, Schloss Rheinach, The Hosps, Feierling, Chef Klaus, Uli, the Rolling Stones, Tamer (Jones) Demirel, Rolf & Anneliese Friedrich, Michaela & Walter, Buddha, the Grateful Dead, Hans Peter, Birgit, Teresa, Meike, Frau Vicary, Universitätsklinik Freiburg Kinder Station, Ilona, Conny and our family in Freiburg and Emmendingen, Germany.

Danny Campbell NZ, Pass de la Sancia, Mark & Inge, BTB Fili & Juan, Shaun and Jeremy R, Vern & Susan, Sefton from Blue Ribbon, Dennis & Peter, Rick Kelly, Carmine Street Guitars, Eddie and the Faicco family.

Roberta's Bushwick: Chris, Eddie, Brandon, Gabe, and our beekeeping community aka Feldman; the big boys: MB, JB, ML, thanks for reviving Italian food to the world for the rest of us to follow.

From Carroll Gardens, Joe and Nick Volpe are the coolest landlords ever; thanks for letting us make our dream come true in your buildings and trusting us to make them beautiful. Thanks to the guys who helped us build Frankies: Richie Godfrey, Rohan, Art Harris, Laredo, Crispo, OGT, Gadi Brimfield, and Joey, and to the guys who still make the neighborhood feel real: Frank Dank, Joe Rock, Mike Pipes, and Larry Love.

I am grateful to our friends and customers, and to Carmine, Tommaso, the Asaro family of Sicily, Allen, Maida Kamco, Jimbolino, Adam Chodos, Amber, Nancy, Amy Lou and Finn, Adie, Cosmo, Sunnys, Antonio Guadagnino, B. Kent, Sarah Bird, CR and Allison, the Black Crowes family, Amie, Cutlets, Dana Bowen, DP, Danny DeVito, Wyckoff Street, Nigro's, Kat and Mike from the stoop, Dario, Darren A., Cole Frates, D. Kahn, D. Pasternak, Greg Ronan, David Sherry, Duane Sorenson & the Stumptown crew, Dustin & Jackie, Elizabeth and Paul Giamatti, Carmen Erbe, Liberatore's, Gerard, Linda & Isabelle Leuci, Jenny B, Joanne & Patrick V., Joe Guido, John Wigmore, Peter & Melinda Kaminsky, Kate Krader, Dana Cowin, Katie & William, Joni Mitchell, the Mulstay, Marci, Michael, Pia, Lily and Hannah Schenk, Liv, Micah, the Vetivers, Ricardo Catania, Scott and Allison, Rob Magnota, Rob and Robin, Ron Gorchov, Santi Moix, Santo Fazzio, Shane Welch, Sarah Rutherford.

I'm grateful to Artisan for letting a group with a vision and little experience in making a book to run with it. Ingrid Abramovitch, Ann Bramson, Jan Derevjanik, Nancy Murray, and Peter Workman: I really want to thank you.

To all our staff at Frankies 457, 17, Prime Meats, and the Pedlar: You make it happen for us day in and day out; we would be nothing without you. Extra-special thanks to Luis Espinosa, Willy Prunty, Greg Fanslau, and the rest of our kitchen crew: you are the lifeblood of this organization.

Travis Lee Kauffman, you are such an inspiration, you never let me down. You're a Frank also. Peter Meehan, you're a wicked great writer. Hats off for putting this book together. Tony Durazzo: Don't ever grow up.

For me, the magic of the Frankies experiences was getting to collaborate with a talented chef, creative thinker, and hilarious person. Thanks, Falcinelli, for being such a driving force.

In loving memory of Louis Dileo Jr., Grandma Lillian, Arthur, Ernie, Josephine, little Annie, Dom Pop, Ann Martucci, Patty Burke, and Jimmy Cincotta.

Last but not least, can't forget to thank the Merle!!

And to anyone we may have forgotten, we are sorry but thank you.

PETER MEEHAN

Frank and Frank and Travis, shaggy madmen all, thanks for roping me into this.

Thanks to Lee & Leah for hipping Ingrid to our long-stalled idea for writing a book, and to Ingrid for thinking it was a good idea and for lighting (and occasionally relighting) the fire under our asses. To Ann Bramson for the encouragement and warmth and good vibes. To Jan Derevjanik and Nancy Murray for their patience. To Suzanne Lander, Barbara Peragine, Erin Sainz, Amy Corley, Chrissa Yee, and Judith Sutton for the hard work that we made harder. (Sorry for the endless headaches.)

To redheaded Sarah Rutherford for the killer drawings! (And her brother Jonathan for pitching in with that meat shoot.)

To Megan Hamilton, who made Spuntino 17 a great place to hang. To Jon Feldman for help on the wine section, and Luis Espinosa for the help in the kitchen, and to Will Prunty for not being insane (comparatively, at least). To all the servers and cooks at Frankies & Prime Meats who have had to deal with me: Sorry. Look, it's over!

To MK & CR for the parties.

Ben Chasny, Elisa Ambrogio, John Shaw, Mr. & Mrs. Spectre Folk and their Violet Ray, Hilly and Duane and the progeny, the Knowlton family, Brian Shebairo, Sameena & Wendy & David, Ibold, Vick and Charlie from Queens, and any of my other friends who came out for photo shoots but didn't end up in the book.

To Kim Witherspoon, as always.

To my parents, who were excited about this one.

To Hazy & Hannah & Evil Little O: forever and ever, amen.

INDEX

NOTE: Page numbers in *italics* refer to illustrations.

A

anchovies 13
  Cannellini, Caper, Lemon & Anchovy
    Crostini 49
  packed in olive oil 13
  Puntarelle with Lemon, Capers, An-
    chovy & Pecorino Romano 80
  Radish Salad with Parsley, Capers &
    Anchovies 85
  Romaine Hearts with Caesar Salad
    Dressing 76–77
antipasto 25–53
  bread and oil 26
  cheese 26, 32–33
  crostini 27, 46–53
  cured meats 26, 29–31, *30*
  olives 27, 28
  plate *26–27*
  vegetables 27, 34–45
apple cider: Mulled Cider 201
artichokes, Jerusalem:
  roasting 43
  roasting for antipasto 35
arugula:
  Arugula, Pecorino & Red Wine Vin-
    aigrette Salad 69
  in mozzarella salad 65
Asaro, Tommaso 18–20, 108
asparagus, roasting 36

avocados:
  Avocado Crostini 50
  growing an avocado tree 210
  Roasted Beet & Avocado Salad ......
    82–83
  shopping for 82
  Tomato, Avocado & Red Onion Salad
    81

B

bacon:
  Bacon, Lettuce & Tomato Sandwich
    57
  Lentil Soup with Smoked Bacon ....
    62–63
basil 23
bay leaves 22
beans:
  Braised Pork Shank with Gigante
    Beans & Rosemary 143–46
  Cannellini, Caper, Lemon & Anchovy
    Crostini 49
  dried 15–16
  Escarole & Cannellini Bean Soup
    60–61
  Gigante Beans 145
  Linguine with Fava Beans, Garlic,
    Tomato & Bread Crumbs ... 106–7

beans *(cont.)*

Pasta Fagiola 60

Roasted Vegetable Salad 72–73

shucking fava beans 106

BeeBo cavatelli makers 3

beef:

Braised Short Ribs 141–42

Meatballs 126–27

Slow-Roasted Rib Eye, Sliced Cold

.... 148

beets:

Roasted Beet & Avocado Salad ......

.... 82–83

Roasted Vegetable Salad 72–73

roasting 37

roasting for antipasto 35

bellinis, fresh fruit 212

beurre noisette 102

blender 2

blowtorch 10

Bocuse, Paul .... xiv, 166

Bouley, David .... xv, 166

Bowen, Dana x

bowls:

mixing 6

salad 66–67

box grater 2–3

braciola:

browning, Grandmas' variation ... 133

butcher's knot *128, 133*

Pork Braciola Marinara 129–33

tying *132, 132*

bread:

and antipasto 26

ciabatta 55

Frankies French Toast 192–93

fresh 13

leftover 13

sandwiches 55, 56–58

stirato 47

Toasts for Crostini 47

bread crumbs 13, 93

Linguine with Fava Beans, Garlic,

Tomato & Bread Crumbs ... 106–7

broccoli rabe:

roasting 38

Sausage & Broccoli Rabe Sandwich

.... 58

broths 13

cheese 14

vegetable 14–15

Brunch 192–93

Frankies French Toast 191–92

Brussels sprouts:

roasting 37

roasting for antipasto 35

Shaved Raw Brussels Sprouts with

Castelrosso 74

Bundt pan 10–11

butcher's knot, tying braciola with .....

.... *128, 132, 133*

butter 13

Hot Buttered Rum 201

C

cacciatorini *30*, 31

Caesar Salad, Romaine Hearts with

Caesar Salad Dressing 76–77

cake: Olive Oil Cake 177

calimari: Grilled Squid 185–86

cannellini beans: *see* beans

can openers 3

capers:

Cannellini, Caper, Lemon & Anchovy Crostini 49

Puntarelle with Lemon, Capers, Anchovy & Pecorino Romano 80

Radish Salad with Parsley, Capers & Anchovies 85

capicola 30–31, *30*

carrots:

Braised Pork Shank with Gigante Beans & Rosemary 143–46

Roasted Vegetable Salad 72–73

roasting 40

roasting for antipasto 35

Castelrosso cheese 205, 207

Shaved Raw Brussels Sprouts with Castelrosso 74

Castronovo 213

Castronovo, Frank:

on bread run xiv

on cooking with kids 209

on crème brûlée 166

and Frankies Spuntino...x, xi, xv–xvii

on Sunday Sauce 153

training in France .... xiv–xv

Castronovo, Heike ....xii, 67

cauliflower:

Roasted Vegetable Salad 72–73

roasting 41

roasting for antipasto 35

cavatelli 90, *91*

Cavatelli with Sausage & Browned Sage Butter...................... 102–4

vegetarian variation, with cauliflower 41

cavatelli makers.................. 3, 90, 101

celery root: Fennel, Celery Root, Parsley & Red Onion Salad with Lemon & Olive Oil 84

cheese 202–8

Amalattea...........................207, 208

antipasto...........................26, 32–33

burrata...............................203, 207

Castelrosso 205, 207

cow...................................204–5, 208

Fiore Sardo............................... 78

Formaggio di Fossa 204, 207

fresh 202–3

goat 208

Gorgonzola 207, 208

grated, with pasta 93

Il Re del Pecorino 204, 207

map of Italy........................... *206–7*

Montasio............................205, 207

mozzarella 202–3

mozzarella di bufala 202–3, 207

Pecorino Romano...........203–4, 207

provolone 204–5, 207

Robiola Bosina..................205, 207

in sandwiches 56

sheep 203–4

stracciatella........................203, 207

Taleggio 207, 208

see also specific cheeses

cheese broth.................................. 14

Linguine Cacio e Pepe 108–9

Semolina Polenta 136

Sweet Potato Ravioli in Cheese Broth .... 110–11 cheesecake:

   crust variation............................ 171

   Ricotta Cheesecake............. 169–71

cheese grater 2, *93*

Chinese five-spice powder 22–23

   Roasted Butternut Squash Soup...59

   Sweet Potato Ravioli in Cheese Broth

   110–11

Chocolate Tart............................. 172

ciabatta 55

cinnamon...................................... 23

Cipollini Onion Vinaigrette 70

   Frankies Greens 71

   Roasted Beet & Avocado Salad ......

   82–83

   Roasted Vegetable Salad 72–73

   Watercress with Fresh Figs & Gor-

   gonzola 75

clam knife 6

Clam Night 188–91

   Baked Clams............................ 190

   shucking clams..... 188–89, *189*, 190

   Spaghetti with Clams................ 191

clean, working.............................. 28

cloves 23

colanders...................................... 9

corn: Frankies Corn Salad 187

crabs 121

   Tony Durazzo's Spaghetti with Crabs

   118–19

Crème Brûlée, Vanilla Bean... 166–67

crème brûlée ramekins 11

cremini mushrooms:

   Cremini Mushroom & Truffle Oil

   Crostini 53

   Roasted Vegetable Salad 72–73

   roasting 42

roasting for antipasto 35

crostini.............................. 46–53

   antipasto................................... 27

   Avocado 50

   Cannellini, Caper, Lemon & Anchovy

   49

   Cremini Mushroom & Truffle Oil

   53

   Parsley Pesto 48

   Ricotta 51

   Roasted Eggplant....................... 52

   Sweet Potato 49

   Toasts....................................... 47

   using leftovers 46

cutting boards.......................2, 3–4

D

dandelion greens, substitute in salads

   80

desserts 165–77

   Chocolate Tart 172

   Hazelnut Panna Cotta 176

   Olive Oil Cake......................... 177

   Pâté Brisée 170–71

   Red Wine Prunes with Mascarpone

   168

   Ricotta Cheesecake............. 169–71

   Tiramisu 173–75

   Vanilla Bean Crème Brûlée...166–67

Durazzo, Tony....xii, *120*, 121, 124–25

   Meatballs Tony's Way 127

   Tony Durazzo's Spaghetti with Crabs

   118–19

E

eggplant:

Eggplant Marinara.............. 137–39

Eggplant Marinara with Mozzarella
Sandwich................................. 58

Grilled Vegetables.................... 186

Quick Eggplant Fix 139

Roasted Eggplant Crostini.......... 52

Sweet-and-Sour Baked Eggplant
with Mint & Ricotta Salata... 140

eggs:

Frankies French Toast......... 192–93

Olive Oil Cake......................... 177

Ricotta Cheesecake............. 169–71

Vanilla Bean Crème Brûlée...166–67

equipment................................. 1–12

blender 2

blowtorch 10

box grater 2–3

can opener................................. 3

cavatelli maker 3

colander.................................... 9

cutting boards 2, 3–4

induction burner .... *xvi*

knives....................................4–6, 7

ladles 6

microplane 2–3

mixers...........................1, 9–10

mixing bowls 6

pasta machine............................. 7

pepper mills........................... 7–8

pots and pans 8–9, 10–11

rolling pin............................... 11

salad spinner............................. 9

scale.. 9

sieve... 9

vegetable peelers......................... 10

whisks 6

escarole:

Escarole & Cannellini Bean Soup...
.... 60–61

Escarole with Sliced Red Onion &
Walnuts 78–79

Everyday Spuntino Menu............ 182

F

Falce 213

Falcinelli, Frank:

and Frankies Spuntino...x, xi, xv–xvii

on Sunday Sauce 154

training in France.................. xiv–xv

a voice from the past ....x–xi

Fennel, Celery Root, Parsley & Red
Onion Salad with Lemon & Olive
Oil.. 84

fettuccine 90, 95

figs: Watercress with Fresh Figs &
Gorgonzola 75

Fiore Sardo cheese, Escarole with
Sliced Red Onion & Walnut.......
.... 78–79

fish:

canned... 13

how to fillet............................. 211

Fleury, Jean 166

flour:

adding to pasta dough........... 94–95

all-purpose 12

semolina................................. 23

Formaggio di Fossa..............204, 207
Frankies Calendar........................ 212
Frankies Corn Salad 187
Frankies Crest............................. 213
Frankies French Toast........... 192–93
Frankies Greens........................... 71
Frankies Lemonade 184
Frankies Olive Oil 18–21
   Linguine with Garlic & Frankies
     Olive Oil 112
Frankies Spuntino ....*xviii*
   birth of............................... xv–xvii
   calendar................................. 212
   crest... 213
   recipes xix
French Toast, Frankies........... 192–93
fruit: fresh fruit bellinis 212

G

garlic...12, 22
   Grilled Vegetables..................... 186
   Linguine with Fava Beans, Garlic,
     Tomato & Bread Crumbs...106–7
   Linguine with Garlic & Frankies
     Olive Oil 112
gnocchi 90, *91*
   Gnocchi Marinara with Fresh Ri-
     cotta....................................... 105
   Potato Gnocchi 98–99
Gorgonzola cheese 207, 208
   Watercress with Fresh Figs & Gor-
     gonzola 75
grapeseed oil 17
graters....................................... 2–3

H

Hazelnut Panna Cotta................ 176
Hellman's mayonnaise 16, 76
herbs.. 22–23
   fresh 23
Hot Buttered Rum 201

I

induction burner........................... *xvi*
Italy, wine and cheese map....... *206–7*

J

Jenkins, Sarah 176
Jerusalem artichokes:
   roasting 43
   roasting for antipasto 35

K

Kauffman, Travis....................xii, 201
kids, cooking with....................... 209
KitchenAid mixers.................... 9–10
Klausman, Michael xii
knives... 4–6
   chef's 4
   clam 6
   palette 7

paring.................................. 4–5
serrated................................ 4
sharpeners 5–6
slicing.................................. 5

L

ladles.................................... 6
Ladner, Mark....................... 168
Lahey, Jim........................... 55
lamb: Tagliatelle with Braised Lamb
   Ragu................................ 113–16
lasagna.................................90, *91*
   Leftovers Lasagna..............163, 164
legumes, dried..................... 15–16
lemon:
   Cannellini, Caper, Lemon & Anchovy
      Crostini 49
   Fennel, Celery Root, Parsley & Red
      Onion Salad with Lemon & Olive
      Oil.............................. 84
   Frankies Lemonade................... 184
   Puntarelle with Lemon, Capers, An-
      chovy & Pecorino Romano 80
   Lentil Soup with Smoked Bacon.......
      62–63
linguine...............................90, *91*
   Linguine Cacio e Pepe 108–9
   Linguine with Fava Beans, Garlic,
      Tomato & Bread Crumbs...106–7
   Linguine with Garlic & Frankies
      Olive Oil 112
   preparing pasta dough................. 95

M

Martucci, Anne......................xvii, 98
mascarpone:
   Red Wine Prunes with Mascarpone
      168
   Tiramisu 173–75
Matsuhisa, Nobu 76
mayonnaise:
   Hellmann's 16, 76
   Romaine Hearts with Caesar Salad
      Dressing 76–77
meatballs...............................*123*
   Leftovers Lasagna..................... 164
   Meatball Marinara Sandwich 58
   the Spuntino Way 126–27
   Tony's Way............................... 127
meat grinders................................. 9
meats 123
   antipasto.....................26, 29–31, *30*
   big cuts................................ 147
   Braised Pork Shank with Gigante
      Beans & Rosemary.......... 143–46
   Braised Short Ribs 141–42
   Meatballs 123, 124–27
   Pork Braciola Marinara.................
      ....128, 129–33
   resting 147
   Roast Center-Cut Pork Chops...149
   in sandwiches 56
   Sausage with Peppers & Onions.....
      134–36
   Slow-Roasted Rib Eye, Sliced Cold
      148
   Summertime Grilling................ 183
   Sunday Sauce 155–56

meat slicer.. *29*

menus for entertaining 181

Brunch 192

Clam Night.............................. 188

Everyday Spuntino Menu 182

Summertime Grilling............... 183

Merlin .... *i*, 213

mesclun 71

microplane 2–3

mint.. 23

Sweet-and-Sour Baked Eggplant
with Mint & Ricotta Salata... 140

mixers 1

stand..................................9–10, 90

mixing bowls................................... 6

Moomba.. x

mozzarella............................... 202–3

in arugula salad 65

Eggplant Marinara.............. 137–39

Eggplant Marinara with Mozzarella
Sandwich................................ 58

Leftovers Lasagna...................... 164

Mozzarella, Tomato & Red Pepper
Sandwich................................ 57

mozzarella di bufala 202–3, 207

Mulled Cider............................... 201

Mulled Wine, Travis's.................. 201

My Bread 55

N

Nutella: Hazelnut Panna Cotta ... 176

nut oils... 17

nuts... 16

O

oils:

and antipasto............................... 26

grapeseed.................................... 17

olive............................... 17–21

pumpkinseed..........................17, 59

sunflower..................................... 17

walnut 17

olive oil 17–21

and antipasto............................... 26

cold-pressed extra-virgin............. 20

Fennel, Celery Root, Parsley & Red
Onion Salad with Lemon & Olive
Oil.. 84

heating 20

Linguine with Garlic & Frankies
Olive Oil 112

Olive Oil Cake........................... 177

using.. 21

olives.. 21

antipasto.................................27, 28

types.. *28*

onions 12

Cipollini Onion Vinaigrette........ 70

Escarole with Sliced Red Onion &
Walnuts 78–79

Fennel, Celery Root, Parsley & Red
Onion Salad with Lemon & Olive
Oil.. 84

Frankies Corn Salad.................. 187

Grilled Vegetables..................... 186

Sausage with Peppers & Onions.....
.... 134–36

Tomato, Avocado & Red Onion Salad
.... 81

Veal Stock 145–46
oranges: Sardine, Blood Orange &
    Puntarelle Salad................. 86–87
orecchiette 90
Orecchiette with Pistachios 117

P

palette knife 7
Palmer, Charlie xv
Panna Cotta, Hazelnut 176
pans:
    baking, rectangular 8
    Bundt 10–11
    half sheet 8
    sheet 8–9
    springform 11
    tart 11
pantry 12–13
    basics 12
    beans and legumes (dried) 15–16
    bread 13
    broths and stocks 13–15
    fish that keep 13
    herbs 22–23
    mayonnaise 16
    nuts 16
    olive oil 17–21
    olives 21
    pasta (dried) 21–22
    seasonings 22–23
    semolina flour 23
    spices 22–23
    tomatoes (canned) 15
    vinegars 17

paring knife 4–5
parsley 22, 23
    Fennel, Celery Root, Parsley & Red
        Onion Salad with Lemon & Olive
        Oil 84
    Radish Salad with Parsley, Capers &
        Anchovies 85
Parsley Pesto 48
    Cannellini, Caper, Lemon & An-
        chovy Crostini 49
pasta 89–121
    Basic Pasta Dough 94–95
    Cavatelli with Sausage & Browned
        Sage Butter 102–4
    cooking 90, 92, 95
    cooking water 92
    dried 21–22, 117–19
    finishing touches 93
    fresh 90, 94–116
    Gnocchi Marinara with Fresh Ri-
        cotta 105
    homemade 90
    Leftovers Lasagna 163, 164
    Linguine Cacio e Pepe 108–9
    Linguine with Fava Beans, Garlic,
        Tomato & Bread Crumbs ... 106–7
    Linguine with Garlic & Frankies
        Olive Oil 112
    Orecchiette with Pistachios 117
    Pasta Dough, Well Method ... 96–97
    Pasta Fagiola 60
    Potato Gnocchi 98–99
    resting 92
    Ricotta Cavatelli 100–101
    saucing 92
    shapes and sizes 91
    Spaghetti with Clams 191

pasta *(cont.)*

and Sunday Sauce 155

Sweet Potato Ravioli in Cheese Broth
.... 110–11

Tagliatelle with Braised Lamb Ragu
.... 113–16

Tony Durazzo's Spaghetti with Crabs
.... 118–19

pasta machine 7, 90, 94–95

pastry equipment 10–11

Pâté Brisée 170–71

Ricotta Cheesecake 169–71

peaches: Watercress Salad variation ...
.... 75

Pecorino Romano 203–4, 207

Arugula, Pecorino & Red Wine
Vinaigrette Salad 69

Cavatelli with Sausage & Browned
Sage Butter 102–4

Cremini Mushroom & Truffle Oil
Crostini 53

Escarole with Sliced Red Onion &
Walnuts 78–79

Gnocchi Marinara with Fresh Ri-
cotta 105

Leftovers Lasagna 164

Linguine Cacio e Pepe 108–9

Linguine with Garlic & Frankies
Olive Oil 112

Prosciutto with Pecorino Sandwich
.... 56

Puntarelle with Lemon, Capers, Anchovy & Pecorino Romano 80

Romaine Hearts with Caesar Salad
Dressing 76–77

pepper 22

pepper mills 7–8

peppers:

Grilled Vegetables 186

Mozzarella, Tomato & Red Pepper
Sandwich 57

roasting 134

Sausage with Peppers & Onions .....
.... 134–36

pesto: Parsley Pesto 48

pine nuts 16

Meatballs 126–27

Semolina Polenta 136

Pintabona, Don 124

pistachios: Orecchiette with Pistachios
.... 117

polenta 23

Semolina Polenta 136

pomegranates, preparing as substitutes
in salad 87

pork:

Braised Pork Shank with Gigante
Beans & Rosemary 143–46

butterflying 130

Pork Braciola Marinara 129–33

steps *128*, 130–33

Pork Ribs 155

Roast Center-Cut Pork Chops ... 149

Sunday Sauce 155–56

Potato Gnocchi 98–99

pots and pans 8–9, 10–11

prosciutto 29, *30*

Prosciutto with Pecorino Sandwich
.... 56

prosecco 195

provolone 204–5, 207

Sopressata with Provolone Sandwich
.... 56

prunes: Red Wine Prunes with Mascarpone 168

pumpkinseed oil 17, 59

puntarelle:

Cannellini, Caper, Lemon & Anchovy
Crostini 49

Puntarelle with Lemon, Capers, Anchovy & Pecorino Romano 80

Sardine, Blood Orange & Puntarelle
Salad.............................. 86–87

R

Radikon, Stanislao 199–200

Radish Salad with Parsley, Capers &
Anchovies............................... 85

raisins: Meatballs 126–27

ramekins 11

ravioli..............................90, *91*

Sweet Potato Ravioli in Cheese Broth
.... 110–11

recipes, about xix

Red Wine Prunes with Mascarpone
.... 168

Red Wine Vinaigrette 68

Arugula, Pecorino & Red Wine
Vinaigrette Salad..................... 69

Reichl, Ruth x

rennet 205

rib eye: Slow-Roasted Rib Eye, Sliced
Cold 148

ricotta:

Gnocchi Marinara with Fresh Ri-
cotta 105

Leftovers Lasagna 164

Radish Salad with Parsley, Capers &

Anchovies............................... 85

Ricotta Cavatelli 100–101

Ricotta Cheesecake............. 169–71

Ricotta Crostini 51

Sweet-and-Sour Baked Eggplant with
Mint & Ricotta Salata........... 140

Robinson, Chris.............................. xi

rolling pin 11

romaine:

Bacon, Lettuce & Tomato Sandwich
.... 57

Romaine Hearts with Caesar Salad
Dressing 76–77

rosé (rosato) wines 196

rosemary 23

Braised Pork Shank with Gigante
Beans & Rosemary.......... 143–46

rum:

Hot Buttered Rum.................... 201

Rum Syrup............................... 173

Tiramisu 173–75

S

sage..22, 23

Cavatelli with Sausage & Browned
Sage Butter....................... 102–4

salad bowls............................... 66–67

salad dressings:

Caesar Salad Dressing........... 76–77

Cipollini Onion Vinaigrette........ 70

Lemon & Olive Oil 84

Puntarelle Dressing.................... 80

Red Wine Vinaigrette................ 68

Walnut Dressing 79

salad greens:
  Frankies Greens 71
  mesclun 71
  storing 66
salads 65–87
  Arugula, Pecorino & Red Wine
    Vinaigrette Salad 69
  Escarole with Sliced Red Onion &
    Walnuts 78–79
  Fennel, Celery Root, Parsley & Red
    Onion Salad with Lemon & Olive
    Oil 84
  Frankies Corn Salad 187
  Frankies Greens 71
  mozzarella and arugula 65
  Puntarelle with Lemon, Capers, An-
    chovy & Pecorino Romano 80
  Radish Salad with Parsley, Capers &
    Anchovies 85
  Roasted Beet & Avocado Salad ......
    82–83
  Roasted Vegetable Salad 72–73
  Romaine Hearts with Caesar Salad
    Dressing 76–77
  Sardine, Blood Orange & Puntarelle
    Salad 86–87
  Shaved Raw Brussels Sprouts with
    Castelrosso 74
  tips 66–67
  Tomato, Avocado & Red Onion Salad
    81
  Watercress with Fresh Figs & Gor-
    gonzola 75
salad spinners 9, 66
salt:
  and pasta 92
  sea 22

salumi, antipasto 26, 31
sandwiches 55–58
  Bacon, Lettuce & Tomato 57
  Eggplant Marinara with Mozzarella
    58
  Meatball Marinara 58
  meat and cheese combos 56
  Mozzarella, Tomato & Red Pepper
    57
  Roasted Vegetable 57
  Sausage & Broccoli Rabe 58
  Sicilian Tuna 57
sardines:
  Cured Sardines 87
  how to fillet 211
  Sardine, Blood Orange & Puntarelle
    Salad 86–87
sauces:
  Browned Sage Butter 102–4
  on pasta 92
  Rum Syrup 173
  Sunday Sauce 155–56
  Tomato Sauce .... xx–xxi
sausages:
  Cavatelli with Sausage & Browned
    Sage Butter 102–4
  Leftovers Lasagna 164
  preparing 102
  real Italian 134
  Sausage & Broccoli Rabe Sandwich
    58
  Sausage with Peppers & Onions .....
    134–36
  Sunday Sauce 155
scales 9
seafood: Summertime Grilling 184
sea salt 22

seasonings 22–23

semolina 23

  Semolina Polenta 136

sharpeners, knife 5–6

sheet pans 8–9

Short Ribs, Braised 141–42

Sicilian Tuna Sandwich 57

sieves 9

soppressata *30*, 31

  Sopressata with Provolone Sandwich
  56

soups 55, 59–63

  cheese broth 14

  Escarole & Cannellini Bean Soup
  60–61

  Lentil Soup with Smoked Bacon ....
  62–63

  Pasta Fagiola 60

  Roasted Butternut Squash Soup ... 59

  veal stock 14

  vegetable broth 14–15

spaghetti 90, *91*

  Spaghetti with Clams 191

  Tony Durazzo's Spaghetti with Crabs
  118–19

speck 29–30, *30*

spices 22–23

springform pan 11

squash:

  Grilled Vegetables 186

  Roasted Butternut Squash Soup ... 59

squid:

  Grilled Squid 185–86

  how to clean 186

stand mixers 9–10, 90

stirato 47

stocks 13

veal 14

String Beans, roasting 44

sugar 12

Sullivan Street Bakery, New York City
  55

Summertime Grilling 183–87

  Frankies Corn Salad 187

  Frankies Lemonade 184

  Grilled Squid 185–86

  Grilled Vegetables 186

  meat 183

  seafood 184

  vegetables 184

sunchokes 43

Sunday Sauce 151–63

  Castronovo on 153

  essentials 155–56

  Falcinelli on 154

  leftovers 163

  pasta 155

  Pork Braciola Marinara 129–33

  salads 155

  the sauce 155–56

  snacks (antipasto) 155

  timeline 157–63

  whole experience of .... xv, 151–52

sunflower oil 17

Sweet-and-Sour Baked Eggplant with
  Mint & Ricotta Salata 140

sweet potatoes:

  roasting 45

  roasting for antipasto 35

  Sweet Potato Crostini 49

  Sweet Potato Ravioli in Cheese Broth
  110–11

T

tagliatelle 90, *91*
  preparing pasta dough................. 95
  Tagliatelle with Braised Lamb Ragu
    113–16
Tart, Chocolate........................... 172
tart pan 11
thyme.. 23
Tiramisu............................... 173–75
Toasts for Crostini........................ 47
tomatoes:
  Bacon, Lettuce & Tomato Sandwich
    57
  buying 81
  canned....................................... 15
  Frankies Corn Salad................. 187
  heirloom..................................... 81
  Linguine with Fava Beans, Garlic,
    Tomato & Bread Crumbs...106–7
  Mozzarella, Tomato & Red Pepper
    Sandwich................................. 57
  Sunday Sauce 155–56
  Sweet-and-Sour Baked Eggplant
    with Mint & Ricotta Salata... 140
  Tagliatelle with Braised Lamb
    Ragu............................... 113–16
  Tomato, Avocado & Red Onion Salad
    81
  Tony Durazzo's Spaghetti with Crabs
    118–19
Tomato Sauce.......................... xx–xxi
  doubling.................................... 156
  Eggplant Marinara.............. 137–39
  Gnocchi Marinara with Fresh Ri-
    cotta....................................... 105

  Meatballs 126–27
  Pork Braciola Marinara....... 129–33
  Sausage with Peppers & Onions.....
    134–36
Tony Durazzo:
  Spaghetti with Crabs 118–19
  Cooking with Tony 121
Tony Durazzo's Spaghetti with Crabs
    118–19
Travis's Mulled Wine 201
truffle oil: Cremini Mushroom &
    Truffle Oil Crostini 53
tuna... 13
  packed in olive oil 13
  Sicilian Tuna Sandwich.............. 57
turnips:
  Braised Pork Shank with Gigante
    Beans & Rosemary.......... 143–46
  Braised Short Ribs 141–42

V

vanilla beans 23
  Vanilla Bean Crème Brûlée...166–67
Veal Stock.........................14, 145–46
vegetable peelers 11
vegetables:
  antipasto...........................27, 34–45
  broth 14–15
  Grilled Vegetables 186
  Roasted Vegetable Salad 72–73
  Roasted Vegetable Sandwich 57
  roasting (guide) 35
  roasting (tip) 34
  Summertime Grilling............... 184

vinaigrettes:
basic 67
Cipollini Onion Vinaigrette 70
emulsified 67
Red Wine Vinaigrette 68
vinegars 17
Vita-Mix blender 2

W

walnut oil 17
walnuts 16
Escarole with Sliced Red Onion &
Walnuts 78–79
Walnut Dressing 79
water:
boiling 92
pasta cooking 92
water buffalos 203
Watercress with Fresh Figs & Gor-
gonzola 75
waterstone 5–6
Well Method for Pasta Dough ....
.... 96–97
whisks 6
wine 194–201
Barbaresco 198–99
Barbera 197–98, 206
Barolo 198–99
Brunello di Montalcino 198
bubbly 195

and cheese, map 206–7
Chianti Classico 198
Friulano 196
Garganega (Soave) 196
Lambrusco 195
Montepulciano 197, 206
Nebbiolo 198–99, 206
Nero d'Avola 197, 206
pairing with food 194–95
pink 196
Pinot Grigio 196
Primitivo 197, 206
red 197–200
Red Wine Prunes with Mascarpone
.... 168
Red Wine Vinaigrette 68
Refrosco 199
Ribolla Gialla 199–200
Rosso di Montalcino 198
Sangiovese 198, 206
Schiava 199
Schiopettino 199
serving temperature 200
Travis's Mulled Wine 201
white 195–96
work clean 28

Z

zucchini: Grilled Vegetables 186
Zyliss Y peeler 11

THE FRANKIES CREST

The star is for inspiration, a guiding light. The downward-pointing star is a symbol of knowledge being passed down to the earthly realm.

The castle represents *Castronovo*, which is Italian for "new castle."

Falce is Italian for "scythe" or "sickle," the root of the name Falcinelli.

Falcinelli adopted his French bulldog, Merlin, a few months before we opened the Spuntino. Merlin was our constant companion in the early days, a bringer of good cheer and good luck. It wasn't long before his little bat-eared head became the logo for the whole enterprise.

The crescent moon set into the crest behind Merlin's head is waxing—going from darkness into light. It's a commonplace symbol in witchcraft and sorcery.

The thirteen leaves on the laurel branches could be a reference to the number of attendees at the Last Supper, or to the original thirteen colonies, or to bad luck. But, for us, the superstition and allegory are an aside. Thirteen is just a powerful, perfect prime number.